Hu

by T.H. Huxley

CONTENTS.

HUME.

PART I.

HUME'S LIFE.

CHAPTER I.

EARLY LIFE: LITERARY AND POLITICAL WRITINGS.

David Hume was born, in Edinburgh on the 26th of April (O.S.), 1711. His parents were then residing in the parish of the Tron church, apparently on a visit to the Scottish capital, as the small estate which his father Joseph Hume, or Home, inherited, lay in Berwickshire, on the banks of the Whitadder or Whitewater, a few miles from the border, and within sight of English ground. The paternal mansion was little more than a very modest farmhouse,[1] and the property derived its name of Ninewells from a considerable spring, which breaks out on the slope in front of the house, and falls into the Whitadder.

Both mother and father came of good Scottish families--the paternal line running back to Lord Home of Douglas, who went over to France with the Douglas during the French wars of Henry V. and VI. and was killed at the battle of Verneuil. Joseph Hume died when David was an infant, leaving himself and two elder children, a brother and a sister, to the care of their mother, who is described by David Hume in My Own Life as "a woman of singular merit, who though young and handsome devoted herself entirely to the rearing and education of her children." Mr. Burton says: "Her portrait, which I have seen, represents a thin but pleasing countenance, expressive of great intellectual acuteness;" and as Hume told Dr. Black that she had "precisely the same constitution with himself" and died of the disorder which proved fatal to him, it is probable that the qualities inherited from his mother had much to do with the future philosopher's eminence. It is curious, however, that her estimate of her son in her only recorded, and perhaps slightly apocryphal utterance, is of a somewhat unexpected character. "Our Davie's a fine goodnatured crater, but uncommon wake-minded." The first part of the judgment was indeed verified by "Davie's" whole life; but one might seek in vain for signs of what is commonly understood as "weakness of mind" in a man who not only showed himself to be an intellectual athlete, but who had an eminent share of practical wisdom and tenacity of purpose. One would like to know, however, when it was that Mrs. Hume committed herself to this not too flattering judgment of her younger son. For as Hume reached the mature age of four and thirty, before he obtained any employment of sufficient importance to convert the meagre pittance of a middling laird's younger brother into a decent maintenance, it is not improbable that a shrewd Scots wife may have thought his devotion to philosophy and poverty to be due to mere infirmity of purpose. But she lived till 1749, long enough to see more than the dawn of her son's literary fame and official importance, and probably changed her mind about "Davie's" force of character.

David Hume appears to have owed little to schools or universities. There is some evidence that he entered the Greek class in the University of Edinburgh in 1723--when he was a boy of twelve years of age--but it is not known how long his studies were continued, and he did not graduate. In 1727, at any rate, he was living at Ninewells, and already possessed by that love of learning and thirst for literary fame, which, as My Own Life tells us, was the ruling passion of his life and the chief source of his enjoyments. A letter of this date, addressed to his friend Michael Ramsay, is certainly a most singular production for a boy of sixteen. After sundry quotations from Virgil the letter proceeds:--

"The perfectly wise man that outbraves fortune, is much greater than the husbandman who slips by her; and, indeed, this pastoral and saturnian happiness I have in a great measure come at just now. I live like a king, pretty much by myself, neither full of action nor perturbation--molles somnos. This state, however, I can foresee is not to be relied on. My peace of mind is not sufficiently confirmed by philosophy to withstand the blows of fortune. This greatness and elevation of soul is to be found only in study and contemplation. This alone can teach us to look down on human accidents. You must allow [me] to talk thus like a philosopher: 'tis a subject I think much on, and could talk all day long of."

If David talked in this strain to his mother her tongue probably gave utterance to "Bless the bairn!" and, in her private soul, the epithet "wake-minded" may then have recorded itself. But, though few lonely, thoughtful, studious boys of sixteen give vent to their thoughts in such stately periods, it is probable that the brooding over an ideal is commoner at this age, than fathers and mothers, busy with the cares of practical life, are apt to imagine.

About a year later, Hume's family tried to launch him into the profession of the law; but, as he tells us, "while they fancied I was poring upon Voet and Vinnius, Cicero and Virgil were the authors which I was secretly devouring," and the attempt seems to have come to an abrupt termination. Nevertheless, as a very competent authority[2] wisely remarks:--

"There appear to have been in Hume all the elements of which a good lawyer is made: clearness of judgment, power of rapidly acquiring knowledge, untiring industry, and dialectic skill: and if his mind had not been preoccupied, he might have fallen into the gulf in which many of the world's greatest geniuses lie buried--professional eminence; and might have left behind him a reputation limited to the traditional recollections of the Parliament house, or associated with important decisions. He was through life an able, clear-headed, man of business, and I have seen several legal documents, written in his own hand and evidently drawn by himself. They stand the test of general professional observation; and their writer, by preparing documents of facts of such a character on his own responsibility, showed that he had considerable confidence in his ability to adhere to the forms adequate for the occasion. He talked of it as 'an ancient prejudice industriously propagated by the dunces in all countries, that a man of genius is unfit for business,' and he showed, in his general conduct through life, that he did not choose to come voluntarily under this proscription."

Six years longer Hume remained at Ninewells before he made another attempt to embark in a practical career--this time commerce--and with a like result. For a few months' trial proved that kind of life, also, to be hopelessly against the grain.

It was while in London, on his way to Bristol, where he proposed to commence his mercantile life, that Hume addressed to some eminent London physician (probably, as Mr. Burton suggests, Dr. George Cheyne) a remarkable letter. Whether it was ever sent seems doubtful; but it shows that philosophers as well as poets have their Werterian crises, and it presents an interesting parallel to John Stuart Mill's record of the corresponding period of his youth. The letter is too long to be given in full, but a few quotations may suffice to indicate its importance to those who desire to comprehend the man.

"You must know then that from my earliest infancy I found always a strong inclination to books and letters. As our college education in Scotland, extending little further than the languages, ends commonly when we are about fourteen or fifteen years of age, I was after that left to my own choice in my reading, and found it incline me almost equally to books of reasoning and philosophy, and to poetry and the polite authors. Every one who is acquainted either with the philosophers or critics, knows that there is nothing yet established in either of these two sciences, and that they contain little more than endless disputes, even in the most fundamental articles. Upon examination of these, I found a certain boldness of temper growing on me, which was not inclined to submit to any authority in these subjects, but led me to seek out some new medium, by which truth might be established. After much study and reflection on this, at last, when I was about eighteen years of age, there seemed to be opened up to me a new scene of thought, which transported me beyond measure, and made me, with an ardour natural to young men, throw up every other pleasure or business to apply entirely to it. The law, which was the business I designed to follow, appeared nauseous to me, and I could think of no other way of pushing my fortune in the world, but that of a scholar and philosopher. I was infinitely happy in this course of life for some months; till at last, about the beginning of September, 1729, all my ardour seemed in a moment to be extinguished, and I could no longer raise my mind to that pitch, which formerly gave me such excessive pleasure."

This "decline of soul" Hume attributes, in part, to his being smitten with the beautiful representations of virtue in the works of Cicero, Seneca, and Plutarch, and being thereby led to discipline his temper and his will along with his reason and understanding.

"I was continually fortifying myself with reflections against death, and poverty, and shame, and pain, and all the other calamities of life."

And he adds very characteristically:--

"These no doubt are exceeding useful when joined with an active life, because the occasion being presented along with the reflection, works it into the soul, and makes it take a deep impression: but, in solitude, they serve to little other purpose than to waste the spirits, the force of the mind meeting no resistance, but wasting itself in the air, like our arm when it misses its aim."

Along with all this mental perturbation, symptoms of scurvy, a disease now almost unknown among landsmen, but which, in the days of winter salt meat, before root crops flourished in the Lothians, greatly plagued our forefathers, made their appearance. And, indeed, it may be suspected that physical conditions were, at first, at the bottom of the whole business; for, in 1731, a ravenous appetite set in and, in six weeks from being tall, lean, and raw-boned, Hume says he became sturdy and robust, with a ruddy complexion and a cheerful countenance--eating, sleeping, and feeling well, except that the capacity for intense mental application seemed to be gone. He, therefore, determined to seek out a more active life; and, though he could not and would not "quit his pretensions to learning, but with his last breath," he resolved "to lay them aside for some time, in order the more effectually to resume them."

The careers open to a poor Scottish gentleman in those days were very few; and, as Hume's option lay between a travelling tutorship and a stool in a merchant's office, he chose the latter.

"And having got recommendation to a considerable trader in Bristol, I am just now hastening thither, with a resolution to forget myself, and everything that is past, to engage myself, as far as is possible, in that course of life, and to toss about the world from one pole to the other, till I leave this distemper behind me."[3]

But it was all of no use--Nature would have her way--and in the middle of 1736, David Hume, aged twenty-three, without a profession or any assured means of earning a guinea; and having doubtless, by his apparent vacillation, but real tenacity of purpose, once more earned the title of "wake-minded" at home; betook himself to a foreign country.

"I went over to France, with a view of prosecuting my studies in a country retreat: and there I laid that plan of life which I have steadily and successfully pursued. I resolved to make a very rigid frugality supply my deficiency of fortune, to maintain unimpaired my independency, and to regard every object as contemptible except the improvement of my talents in literature."[4]

Hume passed through Paris on his way to Rheims, where he resided for some time; though the greater part of his three years' stay was spent at La Fl 飛 he, in frequent intercourse with the Jesuits of the famous college in which Descartes was educated. Here he composed his first work, the Treatise of Human Nature; though it would appear from the following passage in the letter to Cheyne, that he had been accumulating materials to that end for some years before he left Scotland.

"I found that the moral philosophy transmitted to us by antiquity laboured under the same inconvenience that has been found in their natural philosophy, of being entirely hypothetical, and depending more upon invention than experience: every one consulted his fancy in erecting schemes of virtue and happiness, without regarding human nature, upon which every moral conclusion must depend."

This is the key-note of the Treatise; of which Hume himself says apologetically, in one of his letters, that it was planned before he was twenty-one and composed before he had reached the age of twenty-five.[5]

Under these circumstances, it is probably the most remarkable philosophical work, both intrinsically and in its effects upon the course of thought, that has ever been written. Berkeley, indeed, published the Essay Towards a New Theory of Vision, the Treatise Concerning the Principles of Human Knowledge, and the Three Dialogues, between the ages of twenty-four and twenty-eight; and thus comes very near to Hume, both in precocity and in influence; but his investigations are more limited in their scope than those of his Scottish contemporary.

The first and second volumes of the Treatise, containing Book I., "Of the Understanding," and Book II., "Of the Passions," were published in January, 1739.[6] The publisher gave fifty pounds for the copyright; which is probably more than an unknown writer of twenty-seven years of age would get for a similar work, at the present time. But, in other respects, its success fell far short of Hume's expectations. In a letter dated the 1st of June, 1739, he writes,--

"I am not much in the humour of such compositions at present, having received news from London of the success of my Philosophy, which is but indifferent, if I may judge by the sale of the book, and if I may believe my bookseller."

This, however, indicates a very different reception from that which Hume, looking through the inverted telescope of old age, ascribes to the Treatise in My Own Life.

"Never literary attempt was more unfortunate than my Treatise of Human Nature. It fell deadborn from the press without reaching such a distinction as even to excite a murmur among the zealots."

As a matter of fact, it was fully, and, on the whole, respectfully and appreciatively, reviewed in the History of the Works of the Learned for November, 1739.[7] Whoever the reviewer may have been, he was a man of discernment, for he says that the work bears "incontestable marks of a great capacity, of a soaring genius, but young, and not yet thoroughly practised;" and he adds, that we shall probably have reason to consider "this, compared with the later productions, in the same light as we view the juvenile works of a Milton, or the first manner of a Raphael or other celebrated painter." In a letter to Hutcheson, Hume merely speaks of this article as "somewhat abusive;" so that his vanity, being young and callow, seems to have been correspondingly wide-mouthed and hard to satiate.

It must be confessed that, on this occasion, no less than on that of his other publications, Hume exhibits no small share of the craving after mere notoriety and vulgar success, as distinct from the pardonable, if not honourable, ambition for solid and enduring fame, which would have harmonised better with his philosophy. Indeed, it appears to be by no means improbable that this peculiarity of Hume's moral constitution was the cause of his gradually forsaking philosophical studies, after the publication of the third part (On Morals) of the Treatise, in 1740, and turning to those political and historical topics which were likely to yield, and did in fact yield, a much better return of that sort of success which his soul loved. The Philosophical Essays Concerning the Human Understanding, which afterwards became the

Inquiry, is not much more than an abridgment and recast, for popular use, of parts of the Treatise, with the addition of the essays on Miracles and on Necessity. In style, it exhibits a great improvement on the Treatise; but the substance, if not deteriorated, is certainly not improved. Hume does not really bring his mature powers to bear upon his early speculations, in the later work. The crude fruits have not been ripened, but they have been ruthlessly pruned away, along with the branches which bore them. The result is a pretty shrub enough; but not the tree of knowledge, with its roots firmly fixed in fact, its branches perennially budding forth into new truths, which Hume might have reared. Perhaps, after all, worthy Mrs. Hume was, in the highest sense, right. Davie was "wake-minded," not to see that the world of philosophy was his to overrun and subdue, if he would but persevere in the work he had begun. But no--he must needs turn aside for "success": and verily he had his reward; but not the crown he might have won.

In 1740, Hume seems to have made an acquaintance which rapidly ripened into a life long friendship. Adam Smith was, at that time, a boy student of seventeen at the University of Glasgow; and Hume sends a copy of the Treatise to "Mr. Smith," apparently on the recommendation of the well-known Hutcheson, Professor of Moral Philosophy in the university. It is a remarkable evidence of Adam Smith's early intellectual development, that a youth of his age should be thought worthy of such a present.

In 1741 Hume published anonymously, at Edinburgh, the first volume of Essays Moral and Political, which was followed in 1742 by the second volume.

These pieces are written in an admirable style and, though arranged without apparent method, a system of political philosophy may be gathered from their contents. Thus the third essay, That Politics may be reduced to a Science, defends that thesis, and dwells on the importance of forms of government.

"So great is the force of laws and of particular forms of government, and so little dependence have they on the humours and tempers of men, that consequences almost as general and certain may sometimes be deduced from them as any which the mathematical sciences afford us."--(III. 15.) (See p. 45.)

Hume proceeds to exemplify the evils which inevitably flow from universal suffrage, from aristocratic privilege, and from elective monarchy, by historical examples, and concludes:--

"That an hereditary prince, a nobility without vassals, and a people voting by their representatives, form the best monarchy, aristocracy, and democracy."--(III. 18.)

If we reflect that the following passage of the same essay was written nearly a century and a half ago, it would seem that whatever other changes may have taken place, political warfare remains in statu quo:--

"Those who either attack or defend a minister in such a government as ours, where the utmost liberty is allowed, always carry matters to an extreme, and exaggerate his merit or demerit with regard to the public. His enemies are sure to charge him with the greatest enormities, both in domestic and foreign management; and there is no meanness or crime, of which, in their judgment, he is not capable. Unnecessary wars, scandalous treaties, profusion of public treasure, oppressive taxes, every kind of maladministration is ascribed to him. To aggravate the charge, his pernicious conduct, it is said, will extend its baneful influence even to posterity, by undermining the best constitution in the world, and disordering that wise system of laws, institutions, and customs, by which our ancestors, during so many centuries, have been so happily governed. He is not only a wicked minister in himself, but has removed every security provided against wicked ministers for the future.

"On the other hand, the partisans of the minister make his panegyric rise as high as the accusation against him, and celebrate his wise, steady, and moderate conduct in every part of his administration. The honour and interest of the nation supported abroad, public credit maintained at home, persecution restrained, faction subdued: the merit of all these blessings is ascribed solely to the minister. At the same time, he crowns all his other merits by a religious care of the best government in the world, which he has preserved in all its parts, and has transmitted entire, to be the happiness and security of the latest posterity."--(III. 26.)

Hume sagely remarks that the panegyric and the accusation cannot both be true; and, that what truth there may be in either, rather tends to show that our much-vaunted constitution does not fulfil its chief object, which is to provide a remedy against maladministration. And if it does not--

"we are rather beholden to any minister who undermines it and affords us the opportunity of erecting a better in its place."--III. 28.

The fifth Essay discusses the Origin of Government:--

"Man, born in a family, is compelled to maintain society from necessity, from natural inclination, and from habit. The same creature, in his farther progress, is engaged to establish political society, in order to administer justice, without which there can be no peace among them, nor safety, nor mutual intercourse. We are therefore to look upon all the vast apparatus of our government, as having ultimately no other object or purpose but the distribution of justice, or, in other words, the support of the twelve judges. Kings and parliaments, fleets and armies, officers of the court and revenue, ambassadors, ministers and privy councillors, are all subordinate in the end to this part of administration. Even the clergy, as their duty leads them to inculcate morality, may justly be thought, so far as regards this world, to have no other useful object of their institution."--(III. 37.)

The police theory of government has never been stated more tersely: and, if there were only one state in the world; and if we could be certain by intuition, or by the aid of revelation, that it is wrong for society, as a corporate body, to do anything for the improvement of its members and, thereby, indirectly support the twelve judges, no objection could be raised to it.

Unfortunately the existence of rival or inimical nations furnishes "kings and parliaments, fleets and armies," with a good deal of occupation beyond the support of the twelve judges; and, though the proposition that the State has no business to meddle with anything but the administration of justice, seems sometimes to be regarded as an axiom, it can hardly be said to be intuitively certain, inasmuch as a great many people absolutely repudiate it; while, as yet, the attempt to give it the authority of a revelation has not been made.

As Hume says with profound truth in the fourth essay, On the First Principles of Government:--

"As force is always on the side of the governed, the governors have nothing to support them but opinion. It is, therefore, on opinion only that government is founded; and this maxim extends to the most despotic and most military governments, as well as to the most free and the most popular."--(III. 31.)

But if the whole fabric of social organisation rests on opinion, it may surely be fairly argued that, in the interests of self-preservation, if for no better reason, society has a right to see that the means of forming just opinions are placed within the reach of every one of its members; and, therefore, that due provision for education, at any rate, is a right and, indeed, a duty, of the state.

The three opinions upon which all government, or the authority of the few over the many, is founded, says Hume, are public interest, right to power, and right to property. No government can permanently exist, unless the majority of the citizens, who are the ultimate depositary of Force, are convinced that it serves the general interest, that it has lawful authority, and that it respects individual rights:--

"A government may endure for several ages, though the balance of power and the balance of property do not coincide.... But where the original constitution allows any share of power, though small, to an order of men who possess a large share of property, it is easy for them gradually to stretch their authority, and bring the balance of power to coincide with that of property. This has been the case with the House of Commons in England."--(III. 34.)

Hume then points out that, in his time, the authority of the Commons was by no means equivalent to the property and power it represented, and proceeds:--

"Were the members obliged to receive instructions from their constituents, like the Dutch deputies, this would entirely alter the case; and if such immense power and riches as those of all the Commons of Great Britain, were brought into the scale, it is not easy to conceive that the crown could either influence that multitude of people, or withstand that balance of property. It is true, the crown has great influence over the collective body in the elections of members; but were this influence, which at present is only exerted once in seven years, to be employed in bringing over the people to every vote, it would soon be wasted, and no skill, popularity, or revenue could support it. I must, therefore, be of opinion that an alteration in this particular would introduce a total alteration in our government, would soon reduce it to a pure republic; and, perhaps, to a republic of no inconvenient form."--(III. 35.)

Viewed by the light of subsequent events, this is surely a very remarkable example of political sagacity. The members of the House of Commons are not yet delegates; but, with the widening of the suffrage and the rapidly increasing tendency to drill and organise the electorate, and to exact definite pledges from candidates, they are rapidly becoming, if not delegates, at least attorneys for committees of electors. The same causes are constantly tending to exclude men, who combine a keen sense of self-respect with large intellectual capacity, from a position in which the one is as constantly offended, as the other is neutralised. Notwithstanding the attempt of George the Third to resuscitate the royal authority, Hume's foresight has been so completely justified that no one now dreams of the crown exerting the slightest influence upon elections.

In the seventh essay, Hume raises a very interesting discussion as to the probable ultimate result of the forces which were at work in the British Constitution in the first part of the eighteenth century:--

"There has been a sudden and sensible change in the opinions of men, within these last fifty years, by the progress of learning and of liberty. Most people in this island have divested themselves of all superstitious reverence to names and authority; the clergy have much lost their credit; their pretensions and doctrines have been much ridiculed; and even religion can scarcely support itself in the world. The mere name of king commands little respect; and to talk of a king as God's vicegerent on earth, or to give him any of those magnificent titles which formerly dazzled mankind, would but excite laughter in every one."--(III. 54.)

In fact, at the present day, the danger to monarchy in Britain would appear to lie, not in increasing love for equality, for which, except as regards the law, Englishmen have never cared, but rather entertain an aversion; nor in any abstract democratic theories, upon which the mass of Englishmen pour the contempt with which they view theories in general; but in the constantly increasing tendency of monarchy to become slightly absurd, from the ever-widening discrepancy between modern political ideas and the theory of kingship. As Hume observes, even in his time, people had left off making believe that a king was a different species of man from, other men; and, since his day, more and more such make-believes have become impossible; until the maintenance of kingship in coming generations seems likely to depend, entirely, upon whether it is the general opinion, that a hereditary president of our virtual republic will serve the general interest better than an elective one or not. The tendency of public feeling in this direction is patent, but it does not follow that a republic is to be the final stage of our government. In fact, Hume thinks not:--

"It is well known, that every government must come to a period, and that death is unavoidable to the political, as well as to the animal body. But, as one kind of death may be preferable to another, it may be inquired, whether it be more desirable for the British constitution to terminate in a popular government, or in an absolute monarchy? Here, I would frankly declare, that though liberty be preferable to slavery, in almost every case; yet I should rather wish to see an absolute monarch than a republic in this island. For let us consider what kind of republic we have reason to expect. The question is not concerning any fine imaginary republic of which a man forms a plan in his closet. There is no doubt but a popular government may be imagined more perfect than an absolute monarchy, or even than our present constitution. But what reason have we to expect that any such government will ever be established in Great Britain, upon the dissolution of our monarchy? If any single person acquire power enough to take our constitution to pieces, and put it up anew, he is really an absolute monarch; and we have already had an instance of this kind, sufficient to convince us, that such a person will never resign his power, or establish any free government. Matters, therefore, must be trusted to their natural progress and operation; and the House of Commons, according to its present constitution, must be the only legislature in such a popular government. The inconveniences attending such a situation of affairs present themselves by thousands. If the House of Commons, in such a case, ever dissolve itself, which is not to be expected, we may look for a civil war every election. If it continue itself, we shall suffer all the tyranny of a faction subdivided into new factions. And, as such a violent government cannot long subsist, we shall at last, after many convulsions and civil wars, find repose in absolute monarchy, which it would have been happier for us to have established peaceably from the beginning. Absolute monarchy, therefore, is the easiest death, the true Euthanasia of the British constitution.

"Thus if we have more reason to be jealous of monarchy, because the danger is more imminent from that quarter; we have also reason to be more jealous of popular government, because that danger is more terrible. This may teach us a lesson of moderation in all our political controversies."--(III. 55.)

One may admire the sagacity of these speculations, and the force and clearness with which they are expressed, without altogether agreeing with them. That an analogy between the social and bodily organism exists, and is, in many respects, clear and full of instructive suggestion, is undeniable. Yet a state answers, not to an individual, but to a generic type; and there is no reason, in the nature of things, why any generic type should die out. The type of the pearly Nautilus, highly organised as it is, has persisted with but little change from the Silurian epoch till now; and, so long as terrestrial conditions remain approximately similar to what they are at present, there is no more reason why it should cease to exist in the next, than in the past, hundred million years or so. The true ground for doubting the possibility of the establishment of absolute monarchy in Britain is, that opinion seems to have passed through, and left far behind, the stage at which such a change would be possible; and the true reason for doubting the permanency of a republic, if it is ever established, lies in the fact, that a republic requires for its maintenance a far higher standard of morality and of intelligence in the members of the state than any other form of government. Samuel gave the Israelites a king because they were not righteous enough to do without one, with a pretty plain warning of what they were to expect from the gift. And, up to this time, the progress of such republics as have been established in the world has not been such, as to lead to any confident expectation that their foundation is laid on a sufficiently secure subsoil of public spirit, morality, and intelligence. On the contrary, they exhibit examples of personal corruption and of political profligacy as fine as any hotbed of despotism has ever produced; while they fail in the primary duty of the administration of justice, as none but an effete despotism has ever failed.

Hume has been accused of departing, in his old age, from the liberal principles of his youth; and, no doubt, he was careful, in the later editions of the Essays, to expunge everything that savoured of democratic tendencies.

But the passage just quoted shows that this was no recantation, but simply a confirmation, by his experience of one of the most debased periods of English history, of those evil tendencies attendant on popular government, of which, from the first, he was fully aware.

In the ninth essay, On the Parties of Great Britain, there occurs a passage which, while it affords evidence of the marvellous change which has taken place in the social condition of Scotland since 1741, contains an assertion respecting the state of the Jacobite party at that time, which at first seems surprising:--

"As violent things have not commonly so long a duration as moderate, we actually find that the Jacobite party is almost entirely vanished from among us, and that the distinction of Court and Country, which is but creeping in at London, is the only one that is ever mentioned in this kingdom. Beside the violence and openness of the Jacobite party, another reason has perhaps contributed to produce so sudden and so visible an alteration in this part of Britain. There are only two ranks of men among us; gentlemen who have some fortune and education, and the meanest slaving poor; without any considerable number of that middling rank of men, which abound more in England, both in cities and in the country, than in any other part of the world. The slaving poor are incapable of any principles; gentlemen may be converted to true principles, by time and experience. The middling rank of men have curiosity and knowledge enough to form principles, but not enough to form true ones, or correct any prejudices that they may have imbibed. And it is among the middling rank of people that Tory principles do at present prevail most in England."--(III. 80, note.)

Considering that the Jacobite rebellion of 1745 broke out only four years after this essay was published, the assertion that the Jacobite party had "almost entirely vanished in 1741" sounds strange enough: and the passage which contains it is omitted in the third edition of the Essays, published in 1748. Nevertheless, Hume was probably right, as the outbreak of '45 was little better than a Highland raid, and the Pretender obtained no important following in the Lowlands.

No less curious, in comparison with what would be said nowadays, is Hume's remark in the Essay on the Rise of the Arts and Sciences that--

"The English are become sensible of the scandalous licentiousness of their stage from the example of the French decency and morals."--(III. 135.)

And it is perhaps as surprising to be told, by a man of Hume's literary power, that the first polite prose in the English language was written by Swift. Locke and Temple (with whom Sprat is astoundingly conjoined) "knew too little of the rules of art to be esteemed elegant writers," and the prose of Bacon, Harrington, and Milton is "altogether stiff and pedantic." Hobbes, who whether he should be called a "polite" writer or not, is a master of vigorous English; Clarendon, Addison, and Steele (the last two, surely, were "polite" writers in all conscience) are not mentioned.

On the subject of National Character, about which more nonsense, and often very mischievous nonsense, has been and is talked than upon any other topic, Hume's observations are full of sense and shrewdness. He distinguishes between the moral and the physical causes of national character, enumerating under the former--

"The nature of the government, the revolutions of public affairs, the plenty or penury in which people live, the situation of the nation with regard to its neighbours, and such like circumstances."--(III. 225.)

and under the latter:--

"Those qualities of the air and climate, which are supposed to work insensibly on the temper, by altering the tone and habit of the body, and giving a particular complexion, which, though reflexion and reason may sometimes overcome it, will yet prevail among the generality of mankind, and have an influence on their manners."--(III. 225.)

While admitting and exemplifying the great influence of moral causes, Hume remarks--

"As to physical causes, I am inclined to doubt altogether of their operation in this particular; nor do I think that men owe anything of their temper or genius to the air, food, or climate."--(III. 227.)

Hume certainly would not have accepted the "rice theory" in explanation of the social state of the Hindoos; and, it may be safely assumed, that he would not have had recourse to the circumambience of the "melancholy main" to account for the troublous history of Ireland. He supports his views by a variety of strong arguments, among which, at the present conjuncture, it is worth noting that the following occurs--

"Where any accident, as a difference in language or religion, keeps two nations, inhabiting the same country, from mixing with one another, they will preserve during several centuries a distinct and even opposite set of manners. The integrity, gravity, and bravery of the Turks, form an exact contrast to the deceit, levity, and cowardice of the modern Greeks."--(III. 233.)

The question of the influence of race, which plays so great a part in modern political speculations, was hardly broached in Hume's time, but he had an inkling of its importance:--

"I am apt to suspect the Negroes to be naturally inferior to the Whites. There scarcely ever was a civilised nation of that complexion, nor even any individual, eminent either in action or speculation.... Such a uniform and constant difference [between the negroes and the whites] could not happen in so many countries and ages, if nature had not made an original distinction between these breeds of men.... In Jamaica, indeed, they talk of one Negro as a man of parts and learning; but it is likely he is admired for slender accomplishments, like a parrot who speaks a few words plainly."--(III. 236.)

The Essays met with the success they deserved. Hume wrote to Henry Home in June, 1742:--

"The Essays are all sold in London, as I am informed by two letters from English gentlemen of my acquaintance. There is a demand for them; and, as one of them tells me, Innys, the great bookseller in Paul's Churchyard, wonders there is not a new edition, for he cannot find copies for his customers. I am also told that Dr. Butler has everywhere recommended them; so that I hope that they will have some success."

Hume had sent Butler a copy of the Treatise and had called upon him, in London, but he was out of town; and being shortly afterwards made Bishop of Bristol, Hume seems to have thought that further advances on his part might not be well received.

Greatly comforted by this measure of success, Hume remained at Ninewells, rubbing up his Greek, until 1745; when, at the mature age of thirty-four, he made his entry into practical life, by becoming bear-leader to the Marquis of Annandale, a young nobleman of feeble body and feebler mind. As might have been predicted, this venture was not more fortunate than his previous ones; and, after a year's endurance, diversified latterly with pecuniary squabbles, in which Hume's tenacity about a somewhat small claim is remarkable, the engagement came to an end.

FOOTNOTES:

[1] A picture of the house, taken from Drummond's History of Noble British Families, is to be seen in Chambers's Book of Days (April 26th); and if, as Drummond says, "It is a favourable specimen of the best Scotch lairds' houses," all that can be said is worst Scotch lairds must have been poorly lodged indeed.

[2] Mr. John Hill Burton, in his valuable Life of Hume, on which, I need hardly say, I have drawn freely for the materials of the present biographical sketch.

[3] One cannot but be reminded of young Descartes' renunciation of study for soldiering.

[4] My Own Life.

[5] Letter to Gilbert Elliot of Minto, 1751. "So vast an undertaking, planned before I was one-and-twenty, and composed before twenty-five, must necessarily be very defective. I have repented my haste a hundred and a hundred times."

[6] So says Mr. Burton, and that he is right is proved by a letter of Hume's, dated February 13, 1739, in which he writes, "'Tis now a fortnight since my book was published." But it is a curious illustration of the value of testimony, that Hume, in My Own Life, states: "In the end of 1738 I published my Treatise, and immediately went down to my mother and my brother."

[7] Burton, Life, vol. i. p. 109.

CHAPTER II.

LATER YEARS: THE HISTORY OF ENGLAND.

In 1744, Hume's friends had endeavoured to procure his nomination to the Chair of "Ethics and pneumatic philosophy"[8] in the University of Edinburgh. About this matter he writes to his friend William Mure:--

"The accusation of heresy, deism, scepticism, atheism, &c., &c., &c. was started against me; but never took, being bore down by the contrary authority of all the good company in town."

If the "good company in town" bore down the first three of these charges, it is to be hoped, for the sake of their veracity, that they knew their candidate chiefly as the very good company that he always was; and had paid as little attention, as good company usually does, to so solid a work as the Treatise. Hume expresses a naive surprise, not unmixed with indignation, that Hutcheson and Leechman, both clergymen and sincere, though liberal, professors of orthodoxy, should have expressed doubts as to his fitness for becoming a professedly presbyterian teacher of presbyterian youth. The town council, however, would not have him, and filled up the place with a safe nobody.

In May, 1746, a new prospect opened. General St. Clair was appointed to the command of an expedition to Canada, and he invited Hume, at a week's notice, to be his secretary; to which office that of judge advocate was afterwards added.

Hume writes to a friend: "The office is very genteel, 10s. a day, perquisites, and no expenses;" and, to another, he speculates on the chance of procuring a company in an American regiment. "But this I build not on, nor indeed am I very fond of it," he adds; and this was fortunate, for the expedition, after dawdling away the summer in port, was suddenly diverted to an attack on L'Orient, where it achieved a huge failure and returned ignominiously to England.

A letter to Henry Home, written when this unlucky expedition was recalled, shows that Hume had already seriously turned his attention to history. Referring to an invitation to go over to Flanders with the General, he says:

"Had I any fortune which would give me a prospect of leisure and opportunity to prosecute my historical projects, nothing could be more useful to me, and I should pick up more literary knowledge in one campaign by being in the General's family, and being introduced frequently to the Duke's, than most officers could do after many years' service. But to what can all this serve? I am a philosopher, and so I suppose must continue."

But this vaticination was shortly to prove erroneous. Hume seems to have made a very favourable impression on General St. Clair, as he did upon every one with whom he came into personal contact; for, being charged with a mission to the court of Turin, in 1748, the General insisted upon the appointment of Hume as his secretary. He further made him one of his aides-de-camp; so that the philosopher was obliged to encase his more than portly, and by no means elegant, figure in a military uniform. Lord Charlemont, who met him at Turin, says he was "disguised in scarlet," and that he wore his uniform "like a grocer of the train-bands." Hume, always ready for a joke at his own expense, tells of the considerate kindness with which, at a reception at Vienna, the Empress-dowager released him and his friends from the necessity of walking backwards. "We esteemed ourselves very much obliged to her for this attention, especially my companions, who were desperately afraid of my falling on them and crushing them."

Notwithstanding the many attractions of this appointment, Hume writes that he leaves home "with infinite regret, where I had treasured up stores of study and plans of thinking for many years;" and his only consolation is that the opportunity of becoming conversant with state affairs may be profitable:-
-

"I shall have an opportunity of seeing courts and camps: and if I can afterward be so happy as to attain leisure and other opportunities, this knowledge may even turn to account to me as a man of letters, which I confess has always been the sole object of my ambition. I have long had an intention, in my riper years, of composing some history; and I question not but some greater experience in the operations of the field and the intrigues of the cabinet will be requisite, in order to enable me to speak with judgment on these subjects."

Hume returned to London in 1749, and, during his stay there, his mother died, to his heartfelt sorrow. A curious story in connection with this event is told by Dr. Carlyle, who knew Hume well, and whose authority is perfectly trustworthy.

"Mr. Boyle hearing of it, soon after went to his apartment, for they lodged in the same house, where he found him in the deepest affliction and in a flood of tears. After the usual topics and condolences Mr. Boyle said to him, 'My friend, you owe this uncommon grief to having thrown off the principles of religion: for if you had not, you would have been consoled with the firm belief that the good lady, who was not only the best of mothers, but the most pious of Christians, was completely happy in the realms of the just. To which David replied, 'Though I throw out my speculations to entertain the learned and metaphysical world, yet in other things I do not think so differently from the rest of the world as you imagine.'"

If Hume had told this story to Dr. Carlyle, the latter would have said so; it must therefore have come from Mr. Boyle; and one would like to have the opportunity of cross-examining that gentleman as to Hume's exact words and their context, before implicitly accepting his version of the conversation. Mr. Boyle's experience of mankind must have been small, if he had not seen the firmest of believers overwhelmed with grief by a like loss, and as completely inconsolable. Hume may have thrown off Mr. Boyle's "principles of religion," but he was none the less a very honest man, perfectly open and candid, and the last person to use ambiguous phraseology, among his friends; unless, indeed, he saw no other way of putting a stop to the intrusion of unmannerly twaddle amongst the bitter-sweet memories stirred in his affectionate nature by so heavy a blow.

The Philosophical Essays or Inquiry was published in 1748, while Hume was away with General St. Clair, and, on his return to England, he had the mortification to find it overlooked in the hubbub caused by Middleton's Free Inquiry, and its bold handling of the topic of the Essay on Miracles, by which Hume doubtless expected the public to be startled.

Between 1749 and 1751, Hume resided at Ninewells, with his brother and sister, and busied himself with the composition of his most finished, if not his most important works, the Dialogues on Natural Religion, the Inquiry Concerning the Principles of Morals, and the Political Discourses.

The Dialogues on Natural Religion were touched and re-touched, at intervals, for a quarter of a century, and were not published till after Hume's death: but the Inquiry Concerning the Principles of Morals appeared in 1751, and the Political Discourses in 1752. Full reference will be made to the two former in the exposition of Hume's philosophical views. The last has been well said to be the "cradle of political economy: and much as that science has been investigated and expounded in later times, these earliest, shortest, and simplest developments of its principles are still read with delight even by those who are masters of all the literature of this great subject."[9]

The Wealth of Nations, the masterpiece of Hume's close friend, Adam Smith, it must be remembered, did not appear before 1776, so that, in political economy, no less than in philosophy, Hume was an original, a daring, and a fertile innovator.

The Political Essays had a great and rapid success; translated into French in 1753, and again in 1754, they conferred a European reputation upon their author; and, what was more to the purpose, influenced the later French school of economists of the eighteenth century.

By this time, Hume had not only attained a high reputation in the world of letters, but he considered himself a man of independent fortune. His frugal habits had enabled him to accumulate ?,000, and he tells Michael Ramsay in 1751:--

"While interest remains as at present, I have ?0 a year, a hundred pounds worth of books, great store of linens and fine clothes, and near ?00 in my pocket; along with order, frugality, a strong spirit of independency, good health, a contented humour, and an unabated love of study. In these circumstances I must esteem myself one of the happy and fortunate; and so far from being willing to draw my ticket over again in the lottery of life, there are very few prizes with which I would make an exchange. After some deliberation, I am resolved to settle in Edinburgh, and hope I shall be able with these revenues to say with Horace:--

'Est bona librorum et provis?frugis in annum Copia.'"

It would be difficult to find a better example of the honourable independence and cheerful self-reliance which should distinguish a man of letters, and which characterised Hume throughout his career. By honourable effort, the boy's noble ideal of life, became the man's reality; and, at forty, Hume had the happiness of finding that he had not wasted his youth in the pursuit of illusions, but that "the solid certainty of waking bliss" lay before him, in the free play of his powers in their appropriate sphere.

In 1751, Hume removed to Edinburgh and took up his abode on a flat in one of those prodigious houses in the Lawnmarket, which still excite the admiration of tourists; afterwards moving to a house in the Canongate. His sister joined him, adding ?0 a year to the common stock; and, in one of his charmingly playful letters to Dr. Clephane, he thus describes his establishment, in 1753.

"I shall exult and triumph to you a little that I have now at last--being turned of forty, to my own honour, to that of learning, and to that of the present age--arrived at the dignity of being a householder.

"About seven months ago, I got a house of my own, and completed a regular family, consisting of a head, viz., myself, and two inferior members, a maid and a cat. My sister has since joined me, and keeps me company. With frugality, I can reach, I find, cleanliness, warmth, light, plenty, and contentment. What would you have more? Independence? I have it in a supreme degree. Honour? That is not altogether wanting. Grace? That will come in time. A wife? That is none of the indispensable requisites of life. Books? That is one of them; and I have more than I can use. In short, I cannot find any pleasure of consequence which I am not possessed of in a greater or less degree; and, without any great effort of philosophy, I may be easy and satisfied.

"As there is no happiness without occupation, I have begun a work which will occupy me several years, and which yields me much satisfaction. 'Tis a

History of Britain from the Union of the Crowns to the present time. I have already finished the reign of King James. My friends flatter me (by this I mean that they don't flatter me) that I have succeeded."

In 1752, the Faculty of Advocates elected Hume their librarian, an office which, though it yielded little emolument--the salary was only forty pounds a year--was valuable as it placed the resources of a large library at his disposal. The proposal to give Hume even this paltry place caused a great outcry, on the old score of infidelity. But as Hume writes, in a jubilant letter to Clephane (February 4, 1752):--

"I carried the election by a considerable majority.... What is more extraordinary, the cry of religion could not hinder the ladies from being violently my partisans, and I owe my success in a great measure to their solicitations. One has broke off all commerce with her lover because he voted against me! And Mr. Lockhart, in a speech to the Faculty, said there was no walking the streets, nor even enjoying one's own fireside, on account of their importunate zeal. The town says that even his bed was not safe for him, though his wife was cousin-german to my antagonist.

"'Twas vulgarly given out that the contest was between Deists and Christians, and when the news of my success came to the playhouse, the whisper rose that the Christians were defeated. Are you not surprised that we could keep our popularity, notwithstanding this imputation, which my friends could not deny to be well founded?"

It would seem that the "good company" was less enterprising in its asseverations in this canvass than in the last.

The first volume of the History of Great Britain, containing the reign of James I. and Charles I., was published in 1754. At first, the sale was large, especially in Edinburgh, and if notoriety per se was Hume's object, he attained it. But he liked applause as well as fame and, to his bitter disappointment, he says:--

"I was assailed by one cry of reproach, disapprobation, and even detestation: English, Scotch, and Irish, Whig and Tory, Churchman and Sectary, Freethinker and Religionist, Patriot and Courtier, united in their rage against the man who had presumed to shed a generous tear for the fate of Charles I. and the Earl of Strafford; and after the first ebullitions of their fury were over, what was still more mortifying, the book seemed to fall into oblivion. Mr. Millar told me that in a twelvemonth he sold only forty-five copies of it. I scarcely, indeed, heard of one man in the three kingdoms, considerable for rank or letters, that could endure the book. I must only except the primate of England, Dr. Herring, and the primate of Ireland, Dr. Stone, which seem two odd exceptions. These dignified prelates separately sent me messages not to be discouraged."

It certainly is odd to think of David Hume being comforted in his affliction by the independent and spontaneous sympathy of a pair of archbishops. But the instincts of the dignified prelates guided them rightly; for, as the great painter of English history in Whig pigments has been careful to point out,[10] Hume's historical picture, though a great work, drawn by a master hand, has all the lights Tory, and all the shades Whig.

Hume's ecclesiastical enemies seem to have thought that their opportunity had now arrived; and an attempt was made to get the General Assembly of 1756 to appoint a committee to inquire into his writings. But, after a keen debate, the proposal was rejected by fifty votes to seventeen. Hume does not appear to have troubled himself about the matter, and does not even think it worth mention in My Own Life.

In 1756 he tells Clephane that he is worth ?,600 sterling, and consequently master of an income which must have been wealth to a man of his frugal habits. In the same year, he published the second volume of the History, which met with a much better reception than the first; and, in 1757, one of his most remarkable works, the Natural History of Religion, appeared. In the same year, he resigned his office of librarian to the Faculty of Advocates, and he projected removal to London, probably to superintend the publication of the additional volume of the History.

"I shall certainly be in London next summer; and probably to remain there during life: at least, if I can settle myself to my mind, which I beg you to have an eye to. A room in a sober discreet family, who would not be averse to admit a sober, discreet, virtuous, regular, quiet, goodnatured man of a bad character--such a room, I say, would suit me extremely."[11]

The promised visit took place in the latter part of the year 1758, and he remained in the metropolis for the greater part of 1759. The two volumes of the History of England under the House of Tudor were published in London, shortly after Hume's return to Edinburgh; and, according to his own account, they raised almost as great a clamour as the first two had done.

Busily occupied with the continuation of his historical labours, Hume remained in Edinburgh until 1763; when, at the request of Lord Hertford, who was going as ambassador to France, he was appointed to the embassy; with the promise of the secretaryship, and, in the meanwhile, performing the duties of that office. At first, Hume declined the offer; but, as it was particularly honourable to so well abused a man, on account of Lord Hertford's high reputation for virtue and piety,[12] and no less advantageous by reason of the increase of fortune which it secured to him, he eventually accepted it.

In France, Hume's reputation stood far higher than in Britain; several of his works had been translated; he had exchanged letters with Montesquieu and with Helvetius; Rousseau had appealed to him; and the charming Madame de Boufflers had drawn him into a correspondence, marked by almost passionate enthusiasm on her part, and as fair an imitation of enthusiasm as Hume was capable of, on his. In the extraordinary mixture of learning, wit, humanity, frivolity, and profligacy which then characterised the highest French society, a new sensation was worth anything, and it mattered little whether the cause thereof was a philosopher or a poodle; so Hume had a great success in the Parisian world. Great nobles f𝍌 ed him, and great ladies were not content unless the "gros David" was to be seen at their receptions, and in their boxes at the theatre. "At the opera his broad unmeaning face was usually to be seen entre deux jolis minois," says Lord Charlemont.[13] Hume's cool head was by no means turned; but he took the goods the gods provided with much satisfaction; and everywhere won golden opinions by his unaffected good sense and thorough kindness of heart.

Over all this part of Hume's career, as over the surprising episode of the quarrel with Rousseau, if that can be called quarrel which was lunatic malignity on Rousseau's side and thorough generosity and patience on Hume's, I may pass lightly. The story is admirably told by Mr. Burton, to whose volumes I refer the reader. Nor need I dwell upon Hume's short tenure of office in London, as Under-Secretary of State, between 1767 and 1769. Success and wealth are rarely interesting, and Hume's case is no exception to the rule.

According to his own description the cares of official life were not overwhelming.

"My way of life here is very uniform and by no means disagreeable. I have all the forenoon in the Secretary's house, from ten till three, when there arrive from time to time messengers that bring me all the secrets of the kingdom, and, indeed, of Europe, Asia, Africa, and America. I am seldom hurried; but have leisure at intervals to take up a book, or write a private letter, or converse with a friend that may call for me; and from dinner to bed-time is all my own. If you add to this that the person with whom I have the chief, if not only, transactions, is the most reasonable, equal-tempered, and gentleman-like man imaginable, and Lady Aylesbury the same, you will certainly think I have no reason to complain; and I am far from complaining. I only shall not regret when my duty is over; because to me the situation can lead to nothing, at least in all probability; and reading, and sauntering, and lounging, and dozing, which I call thinking, is my supreme happiness--I mean my full contentment."

Hume's duty was soon over, and he returned to Edinburgh in 1769, "very opulent" in the possession of ?,000 a year, and determined to take what remained to him of life pleasantly and easily. In October, 1769, he writes to Elliot:--

"I have been settled here two months, and am here body and soul, without casting the least thought of regret to London, or even to Paris.... I live still, and must for a twelvemonth, in my old house in James's Court, which is very cheerful and even elegant, but too small to display my great talent for cookery, the science to which I intend to addict the remaining years of my life. I have just now lying on the table before me a receipt for making soupe ?la reine, copied with my own hand; for beef and cabbage (a charming dish) and old mutton and old claret nobody excels me. I make also sheep's-head broth in a manner that Mr. Keith speaks of for eight days after; and the Duc de Nivernois would bind himself apprentice to my lass to learn it. I have already sent a challenge to David Moncreiff: you will see that in a twelvemonth he will take to the writing of history, the field I have deserted; for as to the giving of dinners, he can now have no further pretensions. I should have made a very bad use of my abode in Paris if I could not get the better of a mere provincial like him. All my friends encourage me in this ambition; as thinking it will redound very much to my honour."

In 1770, Hume built himself a house in the new town of Edinburgh, which was then springing up. It was the first house in the street, and a frolicsome young lady chalked upon the wall "St. David's Street." Hume's servant complained to her master, who replied, "Never mind, lassie, many a better man has been made a saint of before," and the street retains its title to this day.

In the following six years, the house in St. David's Street was the centre of the accomplished and refined society which then distinguished Edinburgh. Adam Smith, Blair, and Ferguson were within easy reach; and what remains of Hume's correspondence with Sir Gilbert Elliot, Colonel Edmonstone, and Mrs. Cockburn gives pleasant glimpses of his social surroundings, and enables us to understand his contentment with his absence from the more perturbed, if more brilliant, worlds of Paris and London.

Towards London, Londoners, and indeed Englishmen in general, Hume entertained a dislike, mingled with contempt, which was as nearly rancorous as any emotion of his could be. During his residence in Paris, in 1764 and 1765, he writes to Blair:--

"The taste for literature is neither decayed nor depraved here, as with the barbarians who inhabit the banks of the Thames."

And he speaks of the "general regard paid to genius and learning" in France as one of the points in which it most differs from England. Ten years later, he cannot even thank Gibbon for his History without the left-handed compliment, that he should never have expected such an excellent work from the pen of an Englishman. Early in 1765, Hume writes to Millar:--

"The rage and prejudice of parties frighten me, and above all, this rage against the Scots, which is so dishonourable, and indeed so infamous, to the

English nation. We hear that it increases every day without the least appearance of provocation on our part. It has frequently made me resolve never in my life to set foot on English ground. I dread, if I should undertake a more modern history, the impertinence and ill-manners to which it would expose me; and I was willing to know from you whether former prejudices had so far subsided as to ensure me of a good reception."

His fears were kindly appeased by Millar's assurance that the English were not prejudiced against the Scots in general, but against the particular Scot, Lord Bute, who was supposed to be the guide, philosopher, and friend, of both Dowager Queen and King.

To care nothing about literature, to dislike Scotchmen, and to be insensible to the merits of David Hume, was a combination of iniquities on the part of the English nation, which would have been amply sufficient to ruffle the temper of the philosophic historian, who, without being foolishly vain, had certainly no need of what has been said to be the one form of prayer in which his countrymen, torn as they are by theological differences, agree; "Lord! gie us a gude conceit o' oursels." But when, to all this, these same Southrons added a passionate admiration for Lord Chatham, who was in Hume's eyes a charlatan; and filled up the cup of their abominations by cheering for "Wilkes and Liberty," Hume's wrath knew no bounds, and, between 1768 and 1770, he pours a perfect Jeremiad into the bosom of his friend Sir Gilbert Elliot.

"Oh! how I long to see America and the East Indies revolted, totally and finally--the revenue reduced to half--public credit fully discredited by bankruptcy--the third of London in ruins, and the rascally mob subdued! I think I am not too old to despair of being witness to all these blessings.

"I am delighted to see the daily and hourly progress of madness and folly and wickedness in England. The consummation of these qualities are the true ingredients for making a fine narrative in history, especially if followed by some signal and ruinous convulsion--as I hope will soon be the case with that pernicious people!"

Even from the secure haven of James's Court, the maledictions continue to pour forth:--

"Nothing but a rebellion and bloodshed will open the eyes of that deluded people; though were they alone concerned, I think it is no matter what becomes of them.... Our government has become a chimera, and is too perfect, in point of liberty, for so rude a beast as an Englishman; who is a man, a bad animal too, corrupted by above a century of licentiousness. The misfortune is that this liberty can scarcely be retrenched without danger of being entirely lost; at least the fatal effects of licentiousness must first be made palpable by some extreme mischief resulting from it. I may wish that the catastrophe should rather fall on our posterity, but it hastens on with such large strides as to leave little room for hope.

I am running over again the last edition of my History, in order to correct it still further. I either soften or expunge many villainous seditious Whig strokes which had crept into it. I wish that my indignation at the present madness, encouraged by lies, calumnies, imposture, and every infamous act usual among popular leaders, may not throw me into the opposite extreme."

A wise wish, indeed. Posterity respectfully concurs therein; and subjects Hume's estimate of England and things English to such modifications as it would probably have undergone had the wish been fulfilled.

In 1775, Hume's health began to fail; and, in the spring of the following year, his disorder, which appears to have been hemorrhage of the bowels, attained such a height that he knew it must be fatal. So he made his will, and wrote My Own Life, the conclusion of which is one of the most cheerful, simple, and dignified leave-takings of life and all its concerns, extant.

"I now reckon upon a speedy dissolution. I have suffered very little pain from my disorder; and what is more strange, have, notwithstanding the great decline of my person, never suffered a moment's abatement of spirits; insomuch that were I to name the period of my life which I should most choose to pass over again, I might be tempted to point to this later period. I possess the same ardour as ever in study and the same gaiety in company; I consider, besides, that a man of sixty-five, by dying, cuts off only a few years of infirmities; and though I see many symptoms of my literary reputation's breaking out at last with additional lustre, I know that I could have but few years to enjoy it. It is difficult to be more detached from life than I am at present.

"To conclude historically with my own character, I am, or rather was (for that is the style I must now use in speaking of myself, which emboldens me the more to speak my sentiments); I was, I say, a man of mild dispositions, of command of temper, of an open, social, and cheerful humour, capable of attachment, but little susceptible of enmity, and of great moderation in all my passions. Even my love of literary fame, my ruling passion, never soured my temper, notwithstanding my frequent disappointments. My company was not unacceptable to the young and careless, as well as to the studious and literary; and as I took a particular pleasure in the company of modest women, I had no reason to be displeased with the reception I met with from them. In a word, though most men any wise eminent, have found reason to complain of calumny, I never was touched or even attacked by her baleful tooth; and though I wantonly exposed myself to the rage of both civil and religious factions, they seemed to be disarmed in my behalf of their wonted fury. My friends never had occasion to vindicate any one circumstance of my character and conduct; not but that the zealots, we may well suppose, would have been glad to invent and propagate any story to my disadvantage, but they could never find any which they thought would wear the face of probability. I cannot say there is no vanity in making this funeral oration of myself, but I hope it is not a misplaced one; and this is a matter of fact which is easily cleared and ascertained."

Hume died in Edinburgh on the 25th of August, 1776, and, a few days later, his body, attended by a great concourse of people, who seem to have anticipated for it the fate appropriate to the remains of wizards and necromancers, was deposited in a spot selected by himself, in an old burial-ground on the eastern slope of the Calton Hill.

From the summit of this hill, there is a prospect unequalled by any to be seen from the midst of a great city. Westward lies the Forth, and beyond it, dimly blue, the far away Highland hills; eastward, rise the bold contours of Arthur's Seat and the rugged crags of the Castle rock, with the grey Old Town of Edinburgh; while, far below, from a maze of crowded thoroughfares, the hoarse murmur of the toil of a polity of energetic men is borne upon the ear. At times, a man may be as solitary here as in a veritable wilderness; and may meditate undisturbedly upon the epitome of nature and of man--the kingdoms of this world--spread out before him.

Surely, there is a fitness in the choice of this last resting-place by the philosopher and historian, who saw so clearly that these two kingdoms form but one realm, governed by uniform laws and alike based on impenetrable darkness and eternal silence: and faithful to the last to that profound veracity which was the secret of his philosophic greatness, he ordered that the simple Roman tomb which marks his grave should bear no inscription but

DAVID HUME

BORN 1711. DIED 1776.

Leaving it to posterity to add the rest.

It was by the desire and at the suggestion of my friend, the Editor of this Series, that I undertook to attempt to help posterity in the difficult business of knowing what to add to Hume's epitaph; and I might, with justice, throw upon him the responsibility of my apparent presumption in occupying a place among the men of letters, who are engaged with him, in their proper function of writing about English Men of Letters.

That to which succeeding generations have made, are making, and will make, continual additions, however, is Hume's fame as a philosopher; and, though I know that my plea will add to my offence in some quarters, I must plead, in extenuation of my audacity, that philosophy lies in the province of science, and not in that of letters.

In dealing with Hume's Life, I have endeavoured, as far as possible, to make him speak for himself. If the extracts from his letters and essays which I have given do not sufficiently show what manner of man he was, I am sure that nothing I could say would make the case plainer. In the exposition of Hume's philosophy which follows, I have pursued the same plan, and I have applied myself to the task of selecting and arranging in systematic order, the passages which appeared to me to contain the clearest statements of Hume's opinions.

I should have been glad to be able to confine myself to this duty, and to limit my own comments to so much as was absolutely necessary to connect my excerpts. Here and there, however, it must be confessed that more is seen of my thread than of Hume's beads. My excuse must be an ineradicable tendency to try to make things clear; while, I may further hope, that there is nothing in what I may have said, which is inconsistent with the logical development of Hume's principles.

My authority for the facts of Hume's life is the admirable biography, published in 1846, by Mr. John Hill Burton. The edition of Hume's works from which all citations are made is that published by Black and Tait in Edinburgh, in 1826. In this edition, the Essays are reprinted from the edition of 1777, corrected by the author for the press a short time before his death. It is well printed in four handy volumes; and as my copy has long been in my possession, and bears marks of much reading, it would have been troublesome for me to refer to any other. But, for the convenience of those who possess some other edition, the following table of the contents of the edition of 1826, with the paging of the four volumes, is given:--

VOLUME I.

TREATISE OF HUMAN NATURE.

Book I. Of the Understanding, p. 5 to the end

VOLUME II.

TREATISE OF HUMAN NATURE.

Book II. Of the Passions.

Book III. Of Moral

DIALOGUES CONCERNING NATURAL RELIGION.

APPENDIX TO THE TREATISE

VOLUME III.

ESSAYS, MORAL AND POLITICAL.

POLITICAL DISCOURSES

VOLUME IV.

AN INQUIRY CONCERNING HUMAN UNDERSTANDING

AN INQUIRY CONCERNING THE PRINCIPLES OF MORALS.

THE NATURAL HISTORY OF RELIGION

ADDITIONAL ESSAYS

As the volume and the page of the volume are given in my references, it will be easy, by the help of this table, to learn where to look for any passage cited, in differently arranged editions.

FOOTNOTES:

[8] "Pneumatic philosophy" must not be confounded with the theory of elastic fluids; though, as Scottish chairs have, before now, combined natural with civil history, the mistake would be pardonable.

[9] Burton's Life of David Hume, i. p. 354.

[10] Lord Macaulay, Article on History, Edinburgh Review, vol. lxvii.

[11] Letter to Clephane, 3rd September, 1757.

[12] "You must know that Lord Hertford has so high a character for piety, that his taking me by the hand is a kind of regeneration to me, and all past offences are now wiped off. But all these views are trifling to one of my age and temper."--Hume to Edmonstone, 9th January, 1764. Lord Hertford had procured him a pension of ?00 a year for life from the King, and the secretaryship was worth ?000 a year.

[13] Madame d'Epinay gives a ludicrous account of Hume's performance when pressed into a tableau, as a Sultan between two slaves, personated for the occasion by two of the prettiest women in Paris:--

"Il les regarde attentivement, il se frappe le ventre et les genoux ?plusieurs reprises et ne trouve jamais autre chose ?leur dire que Eh bien! mes demoiselles.--Eh bien! vous voil?donc

PART II.

HUME'S PHILOSOPHY.

CHAPTER I.

THE OBJECT AND SCOPE OF PHILOSOPHY.

Kant has said that the business of philosophy is to answer three questions: What can I know? What ought I to do? and For what may I hope? But it is pretty plain that these three resolve themselves, in the long run, into the first. For rational expectation and moral action are alike based upon beliefs; and a belief is void of justification, unless its subject-matter lies within the boundaries of possible knowledge, and unless its evidence satisfies the conditions which experience imposes as the guarantee of credibility.

Fundamentally, then, philosophy is the answer to the question, What can I know? and it is by applying itself to this problem, that philosophy is properly distinguished as a special department of scientific research. What is commonly called science, whether mathematical, physical, or biological, consists of the answers which mankind have been able to give to the inquiry, What do I know? They furnish us with the results of the mental operations which constitute thinking; while philosophy, in the stricter sense of the term, inquires into the foundation of the first principles which those operations assume or imply.

But though, by reason of the special purpose of philosophy, its distinctness from other branches of scientific investigation may be properly vindicated, it is easy to see that, from the nature of its subject-matter, it is intimately and, indeed, inseparably connected with one branch of science. For it is obviously impossible to answer the question, What can we know? unless, in the first place, there is a clear understanding as to what is meant by knowledge; and, having settled this point, the next step is to inquire how we come by that which we allow to be knowledge; for, upon the reply, turns the answer to the further question, whether, from the nature of the case, there are limits to the knowable or not. While, finally, inasmuch as What can I know? not only refers to knowledge of the past or of the present, but to the confident expectation which we call knowledge of the future; it is necessary to ask, further, what justification can be alleged for trusting to the guidance of our expectations in practical conduct.

It surely needs no argumentation to show, that the first problem cannot be approached without the examination of the contents of the mind; and the determination of how much of these contents may be called knowledge. Nor can the second problem be dealt with in any other fashion; for it is only by the observation of the growth of knowledge that we can rationally hope to discover how knowledge grows. But the solution of the third problem simply involves the discussion of the data obtained by the investigation of the foregoing two.

Thus, in order to answer three out of the four subordinate questions into which What can I know? breaks up, we must have recourse to that investigation of mental phenomena, the results of which are embodied in the science of psychology.

Psychology is a part of the science of life or biology, which differs from the other branches of that science, merely in so far as it deals with the psychical, instead of the physical, phenomena of life.

As there is an anatomy of the body, so there is an anatomy of the mind; the psychologist dissects mental phenomena into elementary states of consciousness, as the anatomist resolves limbs into tissues, and tissues into cells. The one traces the development of complex organs from simple rudiments; the other follows the building up of complex conceptions out of simpler constituents of thought. As the physiologist inquires into the way in which the so-called "functions" of the body are performed, so the psychologist studies the so-called "faculties" of the mind. Even a cursory attention to the ways and works of the lower animals suggests a comparative anatomy and physiology of the mind; and the doctrine of evolution presses for application as much in the one field as in the other.

But there is more than a parallel, there is a close and intimate connexion between psychology and physiology. No one doubts that, at any rate, some mental states are dependent for their existence on the performance of the functions of particular bodily organs. There is no seeing without eyes, and no hearing without ears. If the origin of the contents of the mind is truly a philosophical problem, then the philosopher who attempts to deal with that problem, without acquainting himself with the physiology of sensation, has no more intelligent conception of his business than the physiologist, who thinks he can discuss locomotion, without an acquaintance with the principles of mechanics; or respiration, without some tincture of chemistry.

On whatever ground we term physiology, science, psychology is entitled to the same appellation; and the method of investigation which elucidates the true relations of the one set of phenomena will discover those of the other. Hence, as philosophy is, in great measure, the exponent of the logical consequences of certain data established by psychology; and as psychology itself differs from physical science only in the nature of its subject-matter, and not in its method of investigation, it would seem to be an obvious conclusion, that philosophers are likely to be successful in their inquiries, in proportion as they are familiar with the application of scientific method to less abstruse subjects; just as it seems to require no elaborate demonstration, that an astronomer, who wishes to comprehend the solar system, would do well to acquire a preliminary acquaintance with the elements of physics. And it is accordant with this presumption, that the men who have made the most important positive additions to philosophy, such as Descartes, Spinoza, and Kant, not to mention more recent examples, have been deeply imbued with the spirit of physical science; and, in some cases, such as those of Descartes and Kant, have been largely acquainted with its details. On the other hand, the founder of Positivism no less admirably illustrates the connexion of scientific incapacity with philosophical incompetence. In truth, the laboratory is the fore-court of the temple of philosophy; and whoso has not offered sacrifices and undergone purification there, has little chance of admission into the sanctuary.

Obvious as these considerations may appear to be, it would be wrong to ignore the fact that their force is by no means universally admitted. On the contrary, the necessity for a proper psychological and physiological training to the student of philosophy is denied, on the one hand, by the "pure metaphysicians," who attempt to base the theory of knowing upon supposed necessary and universal truths, and assert that scientific observation is impossible unless such truths are already known or implied: which, to those who are not "pure metaphysicians," seems very much as if one should say that the fall of a stone cannot be observed, unless the law of gravitation is already in the mind of the observer.

On the other hand, the Positivists, so far as they accept the teachings of their master, roundly assert, at any rate in words, that observation of the mind is a thing inherently impossible in itself, and that psychology is a chimera--a phantasm generated by the fermentation of the dregs of theology. Nevertheless, if M. Comte had been asked what he meant by "physiologic cerebrale," except that which other people call "psychology;" and how he knew anything about the functions of the brain, except by that very "observation intieure," which he declares to be an absurdity--it seems probable that he would have found it hard to escape the admission, that, in vilipending psychology, he had been propounding solemn nonsense.

It is assuredly one of Hume's greatest merits that he clearly recognised the fact that philosophy is based upon psychology; and that the inquiry into the contents and the operations of the mind must be conducted upon the same principles as a physical investigation, if what he calls the "moral philosopher" would attain results of as firm and definite a character as those which reward the "natural philosopher."[14] The title of his first work, a "Treatise of Human Nature, being an Attempt to introduce the Experimental method of Reasoning into Moral Subjects," sufficiently indicates the point of view from which Hume regarded philosophical problems; and he tells us in the preface, that his object has been to promote the construction of a "science of man."

"'Tis evident that all the sciences have a relation, greater or less, to human nature; and that, however wide any of them may seem to run from it, they still return back by one passage or another. Even Mathematics, Natural Philosophy, and Natural Religion are in some measure dependent on the science of MAN; since they lie under the cognizance of men, and are judged of by their powers and qualities. 'Tis impossible to tell what changes and improvements we might make in these sciences were we thoroughly acquainted with the extent and force of human understanding, and could explain the nature of the ideas we employ and of the operations we perform in our reasonings.... To me it seems evident that the essence of mind being equally unknown to us with that of external bodies, it must be equally impossible to form any notion of its powers and qualities otherwise than from careful and exact experiments, and the observation of those particular effects which result from its different circumstances and situations. And though we must endeavour to render all our principles as universal as possible, by tracing up our experiments to the utmost, and explaining all effects from the simplest and fewest causes, 'tis still certain we cannot go beyond experience; and any hypothesis that pretends to discover the ultimate original qualities of human nature, ought at first to be rejected as presumptuous and chimerical....

"But if this impossibility of explaining ultimate principles should be esteemed a defect in the science of man, I will venture to affirm, that it is a defect common to it with all the sciences, and all the arts, in which we can employ ourselves, whether they be such as are cultivated in the schools of the philosophers, or practised in the shops of the meanest artisans. None of them can go beyond experience, or establish any principles which are not founded on that authority. Moral philosophy has, indeed, this peculiar disadvantage, which is not found in natural, that in collecting its experiments, it cannot make them purposely, with premeditation, and after such a manner as to satisfy itself concerning every particular difficulty which may arise. When I am at a loss to know the effects of one body upon another in any situation, I need only put them in that situation, and observe what results from it. But should I endeavour to clear up in the same manner any[15] doubt in moral philosophy, by placing myself in the same case with that which I consider, 'tis evident this reflection and premeditation would so disturb the operation of my natural principles, as must render it impossible to form any just conclusion from the phenomenon. We must, therefore, glean up our experiments in this science from a cautious observation of human life, and take them as they appear in the common course of the world, by men's behaviour in company, in affairs, and in their pleasures. Where experiments of this kind are judiciously collected and compared, we may hope to establish on them a science which will not be inferior in certainty, and will be much superior in utility, to any other of human comprehension."--(I. pp. 7-11.)

All science starts with hypotheses--in other words, with assumptions that are unproved, while they may be, and often are, erroneous; but which are better than nothing to the seeker after order in the maze of phenomena. And the historical progress of every science depends on the criticism of hypotheses--on the gradual stripping off, that is, of their untrue or superfluous parts--until there remains only that exact verbal expression of as much as we know of the fact, and no more, which constitutes a perfect scientific theory.

Philosophy has followed the same course as other branches of scientific investigation. The memorable service rendered to the cause of sound thinking by Descartes consisted in this: that he laid the foundation of modern philosophical criticism by his inquiry into the nature of certainty. It is a clear result of the investigation started by Descartes, that there is one thing of which no doubt can be entertained, for he who should pretend to doubt it would thereby prove its existence; and that is the momentary consciousness we call a present thought or feeling; that is safe, even if all other kinds of certainty are merely more or less probable inferences. Berkeley and Locke, each in his way, applied philosophical criticism in other directions; but they always, at any rate professedly, followed the Cartesian maxim of admitting no propositions to be true but such as are clear, distinct, and evident, even while their arguments stripped off many a layer of hypothetical assumption which their great predecessor had left untouched. No one has more clearly stated the aims of the critical philosopher than Locke, in a passage of the famous Essay concerning Human Understanding, which, perhaps, I ought to assume to be well known to all English readers, but which so probably is unknown to this full-crammed and much examined generation that I venture to cite it:

"If by this inquiry into the nature of the understanding I can discover the powers thereof, how far they reach, to what things they are in any degree proportionate, and where they fail us, I suppose it may be of use to prevail with the busy mind of man to be more cautious in meddling with things exceeding its comprehension: to stop when it is at the utmost extent of its tether; and to sit down in quiet ignorance of those things which, upon examination, are proved to be beyond the reach of our capacities. We should not then, perhaps, be so forward, out of an affectation of universal knowledge, to raise questions and perplex ourselves and others with disputes about things to which our understandings are not suited, and of which we cannot frame in our minds any clear and distinct perception, or whereof (as it has, perhaps, too often happened) we have not any notion at all.... Men may find matter sufficient to busy their heads and employ their hands with variety, delight, and satisfaction, if they will not boldly quarrel with their own constitution and throw away the blessings their hands are filled with because they are not big enough to grasp everything. We shall not have much reason to complain of the narrowness of our minds, if we will but employ them about what may be of use to us: for of that they are very capable: and it will be an unpardonable, as well as a childish peevishness, if we under-value the advantages of our knowledge, and neglect to improve it to the ends for which it was given us, because there are some things that are set out of the reach of it. It will be no excuse to an idle and untoward servant who would not attend to his business by candlelight, to plead that he had not broad sunshine. The candle that is set up in us shines bright enough for all our purposes.... Our business here is not to know all things, but those which concern our conduct."[16]

Hume develops the same fundamental conception in a somewhat different way, and with a more definite indication of the practical benefits which may be expected from a critical philosophy. The first and second parts of the twelfth section of the Inquiry are devoted to a condemnation of excessive scepticism, or Pyrrhonism, with which Hume couples a caricature of the Cartesian doubt; but, in the third part, a certain "mitigated scepticism" is recommended and adopted, under the title of "academical philosophy." After pointing out that a knowledge of the infirmities of the human understanding, even in its most perfect state, and when most accurate and cautious in its determinations, is the best check upon the tendency to dogmatism, Hume continues:--

"Another species of mitigated scepticism, which may be of advantage to mankind, and which maybe the natural result of the PYRRHONIAN doubts and scruples, is the limitation of our inquiries to such subjects as are best adapted to the narrow capacity of human understanding. The imagination of man is naturally sublime, delighted with whatever is remote and extraordinary, and running, without control, into the most distant parts of space and time in order to avoid the objects which custom has rendered too familiar to it. A correct judgment observes a contrary method, and, avoiding all distant and high inquiries, confines itself to common life, and to such subjects as fall under daily practice and experience; leaving the more sublime topics to the embellishment of poets and orators, or to the arts of priests and politicians.

To bring us to so salutary a determination, nothing can be more serviceable than to be once thoroughly convinced of the force of the PYRRHONIAN doubt, and of the impossibility that anything but the strong power of natural instinct could free us from it. Those who have a propensity to philosophy will still continue their researches; because they reflect, that, besides the immediate pleasure attending such an occupation, philosophical decisions are nothing but the reflections of common life, methodised and corrected. But they will never be tempted to go beyond common life, so long as they consider the imperfection of those faculties which they employ, their narrow reach, and their inaccurate operations. While we cannot give a satisfactory reason why we believe, after a thousand experiments, that a stone will fall or fire burn; can we ever satisfy ourselves concerning any determination which we may form with regard to the origin of worlds and the situation of nature from and to eternity?"--(IV. pp. 189--90.)

But further, it is the business of criticism not only to keep watch over the vagaries of philosophy, but to do the duty of police in the whole world of thought. Wherever it espies sophistry or superstition they are to be bidden to stand; nay, they are to be followed to their very dens and there apprehended and exterminated, as Othello smothered Desdemona, "else she'll betray more men."

Hume warms into eloquence as he sets forth the labours meet for the strength and the courage of the Hercules of "mitigated scepticism."

"Here, indeed, lies the justest and most plausible objection against a considerable part of metaphysics, that they are not properly a science, but arise either from the fruitless efforts of human vanity, which would penetrate into subjects utterly inaccessible to the understanding, or from the craft of popular superstitions, which, being unable to defend themselves on fair ground, raise these entangling brambles to cover and protect their weakness. Chased from the open country, these robbers fly into the forest, and lie in wait to break in upon every unguarded avenue of the mind and overwhelm it with religious fears and prejudices. The stoutest antagonist, if he remits his watch a moment, is oppressed; and many, through cowardice and folly, open the gates to the enemies, and willingly receive them with reverence and submission as their legal sovereigns.

"But is this a sufficient reason why philosophers should desist from such researches and leave superstition still in possession of her retreat? Is it not proper to draw an opposite conclusion, and perceive the necessity of carrying the war into the most secret recesses of the enemy?... The only method of freeing learning at once from these abstruse questions, is to inquire seriously into the nature of human understanding, and show, from an exact analysis of its powers and capacity, that it is by no means fitted for such remote and abstruse subjects. We must submit to this fatigue, in order to live at ease ever after; and must cultivate true metaphysics with some care, in order to destroy the false and adulterated."--(IV. pp. 10, 11.)

Near a century and a half has elapsed since these brave words were shaped by David Hume's pen; and the business of carrying the war into the enemy's camp has gone on but slowly. Like other campaigns, it long languished for want of a good base of operations. But since physical science, in the course of the last fifty years, has brought to the front an inexhaustible supply of heavy artillery of a new pattern, warranted to drive solid bolts of fact through the thickest skulls, things are looking better; though hardly more than the first faint flutterings of the dawn of the happy day, when superstition and false metaphysics shall be no more and reasonable folks may "live at ease," are as yet discernible by the enfants perdus of the outposts.

If, in thus conceiving the object and the limitations of philosophy, Hume shows himself the spiritual child and continuator of the work of Locke, he appears no less plainly as the parent of Kant and as the protagonist of that more modern way of thinking, which has been called "agnosticism," from its profession of an incapacity to discover the indispensable conditions of either positive or negative knowledge, in many propositions, respecting which, not only the vulgar, but philosophers of the more sanguine sort, revel in the luxury of unqualified assurance.

The aim of the Kritik der reinen Vernunft is essentially the same as that of the Treatise of Human Nature, by which indeed Kant was led to develop that "critical philosophy" with which his name and fame are indissolubly bound up: and, if the details of Kant's criticism differ from those of Hume, they coincide with them in their main result, which is the limitation of all knowledge of reality to the world of phenomena revealed to us by experience.

The philosopher of Konigsberg epitomises the philosopher of Ninewells when he thus sums up the uses of philosophy:--

"The greatest and perhaps the sole use of all philosophy of pure reason is, after all, merely negative, since it serves, not as an organon for the enlargement [of knowledge], but as a discipline for its delimitation; and instead of discovering truth, has only the modest merit of preventing error."[17]

FOOTNOTES:

[14] In a letter to Hutcheson (September 17th, 1739) Hume remarks:-- "There are different ways of examining the mind as well as the body. One may consider it either as an anatomist or as a painter: either to discover its most secret springs and principles, or to describe the grace and beauty of its actions;" and he proceeds to justify his own mode of looking at the moral sentiments from the anatomist's point of view.

[15] The manner in which Hume constantly refers to the results of the observation of the contents and the processes of his own mind clearly shows that he has here inadvertently overstated the case.

[16] Locke, An Essay concerning Human Understanding, Book I, chap. i, Ë 4, 5, 6.

[17] Kritik der reinen Vernunft. Ed. Hartenstein, p. 256.

CHAPTER II.

THE CONTENTS OF THE MIND.

In the language of common life, the "mind" is spoken of as an entity, independent of the body, though resident in and closely connected with it, and endowed with numerous "faculties," such as sensibility, understanding, memory, volition, which stand in the same relation to the mind as the organs do to the body, and perform the functions of feeling, reasoning, remembering, and willing. Of these functions, some, such as sensation, are supposed to be merely passive--that is, they are called into existence by impressions, made upon the sensitive faculty by a material world of real objects, of which our sensations are supposed to give us pictures; others, such as the memory and the reasoning faculty, are considered to be partly passive and partly active; while volition is held to be potentially, if not always actually, a spontaneous activity.

The popular classification and terminology of the phenomena of consciousness, however, are by no means the first crude conceptions suggested by common sense, but rather a legacy, and, in many respects, a sufficiently damnosa hereditas, of ancient philosophy, more or less leavened by theology; which has incorporated itself with the common thought of later times, as the vices of the aristocracy of one age become those of the mob in the next. Very little attention to what passes in the mind is sufficient to show, that these conceptions involve assumptions of an extremely hypothetical character. And the first business of the student of psychology is to get rid of such prepossessions; to form conceptions of mental phenomena as they are given us by observation, without any hypothetical admixture, or with only so much as is definitely recognised and held subject to confirmation or otherwise; to classify these phenomena according to their clearly recognisable characters; and to adopt a nomenclature which suggests nothing beyond the results of observation. Thus chastened, observation of the mind makes us acquainted with nothing but certain events, facts, or phenomena (whichever name be preferred) which pass over the inward field of view in rapid and, as it may appear on careless inspection, in disorderly succession, like the shifting patterns of a kaleidoscope. To all these mental phenomena, or states of our consciousness,[18] Descartes gave the name of "thoughts,"[19] while Locke and Berkeley termed them "ideas." Hume, regarding this as an improper use of the word "idea," for which he proposes another employment, gives the general name of "perceptions" to all states of consciousness. Thus, whatever other signification we may see reason to attach to the word "mind," it is certain that it is a name which is employed to denote a series of perceptions; just as the word "tune," whatever else it may mean, denotes, in the first place, a succession of musical notes. Hume, indeed, goes further than others when he says that--

"What we call a mind is nothing but a heap or collection of different perceptions, united together by certain relations, and supposed, though falsely, to be endowed with a perfect simplicity and identity."--(I. p. 268.)

With this "nothing but," however, he obviously falls into the primal and perennial error of philosophical speculators--dogmatising from negative arguments. He may be right or wrong; but the most he, or anybody else, can prove in favour of his conclusion is, that we know nothing more of the mind than that it is a series of perceptions. Whether there is something in the mind that lies beyond the reach of observation; or whether perceptions themselves are the products of something which can be observed and which is not mind; are questions which can in nowise be settled by direct observation. Elsewhere, the objectionable hypothetical element of the definition of mind is less prominent:--

"The true idea of the human mind is to consider it as a system of different perceptions, or different existences, which are linked together by the relation of cause and effect, and mutually produce, destroy, influence and modify each other.... In this respect I cannot compare the soul more properly to anything than a republic or commonwealth, in which the several members are united by the reciprocal ties of government and subordination, and give rise to other persons who propagate the same republic in the incessant changes of its parts."--(I. p. 331).

But, leaving the question of the proper definition of mind open for the present, it is further a matter of direct observation, that, when we take a general survey of all our perceptions or states of consciousness, they naturally fall into sundry groups or classes. Of these classes, two are distinguished by Hume as of primary importance. All "perceptions," he says, are either "Impressions" or "Ideas."

Under "impressions" he includes "all our more lively perceptions, when we hear, see, feel, love, or will;" in other words, "all our sensations, passions, and emotions, as they make their first appearance in the soul" (I. p. 15).

"Ideas," on the other hand, are the faint images of impressions in thinking and reasoning, or of antecedent ideas.

Both impressions and ideas may be either simple, when they are incapable of further analysis, or complex, when they may be resolved into simpler constituents. All simple ideas are exact copies of impressions; but, in complex ideas, the arrangement of simple constituents may be different from that of the impressions of which those simple ideas are copies.

Thus the colours red and blue and the odour of a rose, are simple impressions; while the ideas of blue, of red, and of rose-odour are simple copies of these impressions. But a red rose gives us a complex impression, capable of resolution into the simple impressions of red colour, rose-scent, and numerous others; and we may have a complex idea, which is an accurate, though faint, copy of this complex impression. Once in possession of the ideas of a red rose and of the colour blue, we may, in imagination, substitute blue for red; and thus obtain a complex idea of a blue rose, which is not an actual copy of any complex impression, though all its elements are such copies.

Hume has been criticised for making the distinction of impressions and ideas to depend upon their relative strength or vivacity. Yet it would be hard to point out any other character by which the things signified can be distinguished. Any one who has paid attention to the curious subject of what are called "subjective sensations" will be familiar with examples of the extreme difficulty which sometimes attends the discrimination of ideas of sensation from impressions of sensation, when the ideas are very vivid, or the impressions are faint. Who has not "fancied" he heard a noise; or has not explained inattention to a real sound by saying, "I thought it was nothing but my fancy"? Even healthy persons are much more liable to both visual and auditory spectra--that is, ideas of vision and sound so vivid that they are taken for new impressions--than is commonly supposed; and, in some diseased states, ideas of sensible objects may assume all the vividness of reality.

If ideas are nothing but copies of impressions, arranged, either in the same order as that of the impressions from which they are derived, or in a different order, it follows that the ultimate analysis of the contents of the mind turns upon that of the impressions. According to Hume, these are of two kinds: either they are impressions of sensation, or they are impressions of reflection. The former are those afforded by the five senses, together with pleasure and pain. The latter are the passions or the emotions (which Hume employs as equivalent terms). Thus the elementary states of consciousness, the raw materials of knowledge, so to speak, are either sensations or emotions; and whatever we discover in the mind, beyond these elementary states of consciousness, results from the combinations and the metamorphoses which they undergo.

It is not a little strange that a thinker of Hume's capacity should have been satisfied with the results of a psychological analysis which regards some obvious compounds as elements, while it omits altogether a most important class of elementary states.

With respect to the former point, Spinoza's masterly examination of the Passions in the third part of the Ethics should have been known to Hume.[20] But, if he had been acquainted with that wonderful piece of psychological anatomy, he would have learned that the emotions and passions are all complex states, arising from the close association of ideas of pleasure or pain with other ideas; and, indeed, without going to Spinoza, his own acute discussion of the passions leads to the same result,[21] and is wholly inconsistent with his classification of those mental states among the primary uncompounded materials of consciousness.

If Hume's "impressions of reflection" are excluded from among the primary elements of consciousness, nothing is left but the impressions afforded by the five senses, with pleasure and pain. Putting aside the muscular sense, which had not come into view in Hume's time, the questions arise whether these are all the simple undecomposable materials of thought? or whether others exist of which Hume takes no cognizance.

Kant answered the latter question in the affirmative, in the Kritik der reinen Vernunft, and thereby made one of the greatest advances ever effected in philosophy; though it must be confessed that the German philosopher's exposition of his views is so perplexed in style, so burdened with the weight of a cumbrous and uncouth scholasticism, that it is easy to confound the unessential parts of his system with those which are of profound importance. His baggage train is bigger than his army, and the student who attacks him is too often led to suspect he has won a position when he has only captured a mob of useless camp-followers.

In his Principles of Psychology, Mr. Herbert Spencer appears to me to have brought out the essential truth which underlies Kant's doctrine in a far clearer manner than any one else; but, for the purpose of the present summary view of Hume's philosophy, it must suffice if I state the matter in my own way, giving the broad outlines, without entering into the details of a large and difficult discussion.

When a red light flashes across the field of vision, there arises in the mind an "impression of sensation"--which we call red. It appears to me that this sensation, red, is a something which may exist altogether independently of any other impression, or idea, as an individual existence. It is perfectly conceivable that a sentient being should have no sense but vision, and that he should have spent his existence in absolute darkness, with the exception of one solitary flash of red light. That momentary illumination would suffice to give him the impression under consideration; and the whole content of his consciousness might be that impression; and, if he were endowed with memory, its idea.

Such being the state of affairs, suppose a second flash of red light to follow the first. If there were no memory of the latter, the state of the mind on the second occasion would simply be a repetition of that which occurred before. There would be merely another impression.

But suppose memory to exist, and that an idea of the first impression is generated; then, if the supposed sentient being were like ourselves, there might arise in his mind two altogether new impressions. The one is the feeling of the succession of the two impressions, the other is the feeling of their similarity.

Yet a third case is conceivable. Suppose two flashes of red light to occur together, then a third feeling might arise which is neither succession nor similarity, but that which we call co-existence.

These feelings, or their contraries, are the foundation of everything that we call a relation. They are no more capable of being described than sensations are; and, as it appears to me, they are as little susceptible of analysis into simpler elements. Like simple tastes and smells, or feelings of pleasure and pain, they are ultimate irresolvable facts of conscious experience; and, if we follow the principle of Hume's nomenclature, they must be called impressions of relation. But it must be remembered, that they differ from the other impressions, in requiring the pre-existence of at least two of the latter. Though devoid of the slightest resemblance to the other impressions, they are, in a manner, generated by them. In fact, we may regard them as a kind of impressions of impressions; or as the sensations of an inner sense, which takes cognizance of the materials furnished to it by the outer senses.

Hume failed as completely as his predecessors had done to recognise the elementary character of impressions of relation; and, when he discusses relations, he falls into a chaos of confusion and self-contradiction.

In the Treatise, for example, (Book I., ?iv.) resemblance, contiguity in time and space, and cause and effect, are said to be the "uniting principles among ideas," "the bond of union" or "associating quality by which one idea naturally introduces another." Hume affirms that--

"These qualities produce an association among ideas, and upon the appearance of one idea naturally introduce another." They are "the principles of union or cohesion among our simple ideas, and, in the imagination, supply the place of that inseparable connection by which they are united in our memory. Here is a kind of attraction, which, in the mental world, will be found to have as extraordinary effects as in the natural, and to show itself in as many and as various forms. Its effects are everywhere conspicuous; but, as to its causes they are mostly unknown, and must be resolved into original qualities of human nature, which I pretend not to explain."--(I. p. 29.)

And at the end of this section Hume goes on to say--

"Amongst the effects of this union or association of ideas, there are none more remarkable than those complex ideas which are the common subjects of our thought and reasoning, and generally arise from some principle of union among our simple ideas. These complex ideas may be resolved into relations, modes, and substances."--(Ibid.)

In the next section, which is devoted to Relations, they are spoken of as qualities "by which two ideas are connected together in the imagination," or "which make objects admit of comparison," and seven kinds of relation are enumerated, namely, resemblance, identity, space and time, quantity or number, degrees of quality, contrariety, and cause and effect.

To the reader of Hume, whose conceptions are usually so clear, definite, and consistent, it is as unsatisfactory as it is surprising to meet with so much questionable and obscure phraseology in a small space. One and the same thing, for example, resemblance, is first called a "quality of an idea," and secondly a "complex idea." Surely it cannot be both. Ideas which have the qualities of "resemblance, contiguity, and cause and effect," are said to "attract one another" (save the mark!), and so become associated; though, in a subsequent part of the Treatise, Hume's great effort is to prove that the relation of cause and effect is a particular case of the process of association; that is to say, is a result of the process of which it is supposed to be the cause. Moreover, since, as Hume is never weary of reminding his readers, there is nothing in ideas save copies of impressions, the qualities of resemblance, contiguity, and so on, in the idea, must have existed in the impression of which that idea is a copy; and therefore they must be either sensations or emotions--from both of which classes they are excluded.

In fact, in one place, Hume himself has an insight into the real nature of relations. Speaking of equality, in the sense of a relation of quantity, he says--

"Since equality is a relation, it is not, strictly speaking, a property in the figures themselves, but arises merely from the comparison which the mind makes between them."--(I. p. 70.)

That is to say, when two impressions of equal figures are present, there arises in the mind a tertium quid, which is the perception of equality. On his own principles, Hume should therefore have placed this "perception" among the ideas of reflection. However, as we have seen, he expressly excludes everything but the emotions and the passions from this group.

It is necessary therefore to amend Hume's primary "geography of the mind" by the excision of one territory and the addition of another; and the elementary states of consciousness will stand thus:--

A. IMPRESSIONS. A. Sensations of a. Smell. b. Taste. c. Hearing. d. Sight. e. Touch. f. Resistance (the muscular sense). B. Pleasure and Pain. C. Relations. a. Co-existence. b. Succession. c. Similarity and dissimilarity. B. IDEAS. Copies, or reproductions in memory, of the foregoing.

And now the question arises, whether any, and if so what, portion of these contents of the mind are to be termed "knowledge."

According to Locke, "Knowledge is the perception of the agreement or disagreement of two ideas;" and Hume, though he does not say so in so many words, tacitly accepts the definition. It follows, that neither simple sensation, nor simple emotion, constitutes knowledge; but that, when impressions of relation are added to these impressions, or their ideas, knowledge arises; and that all knowledge is the knowledge of likenesses and unlikenesses, co-existences and successions.

It really matters very little in what sense terms are used, so long as the same meaning is always rigidly attached to them; and, therefore, it is hardly worth while to quarrel with this generally accepted, though very arbitrary, limitation of the signification of "knowledge." But, on the face of the matter, it is not obvious why the impression we call a relation should have a better claim to the title of knowledge, than that which we call a sensation or an emotion; and the restriction has this unfortunate result, that it excludes all the most intense states of consciousness from any claim to the title of "knowledge."

For example, on this view, pain, so violent and absorbing as to exclude all other forms of consciousness, is not knowledge; but becomes a part of knowledge the moment we think of it in relation to another pain, or to some other mental phenomenon. Surely this is somewhat inconvenient, for there is only a verbal difference between having a sensation and knowing one has it: they are simply two phrases for the same mental state.

But the "pure metaphysicians" make great capital out of the ambiguity. For, starting with the assumption that all knowledge is the perception of relations, and finding themselves, like mere common-sense folks, very much disposed to call sensation knowledge, they at once gratify that disposition and save their consistency, by declaring that even the simplest act of sensation contains two terms and a relation--the sensitive subject, the sensigenous object, and that masterful entity, the Ego. From which great triad, as from a gnostic Trinity, emanates an endless procession of other logical shadows and all the Fata Morgana of philosophical dreamland.

FOOTNOTES:

[18] "Consciousnesses" would be a better name, but it is awkward. I have elsewhere proposed psychoses as a substantive name for mental phenomena.

[19] As this has been denied, it may be as well to give Descartes's words: "Par le mot de penser, j'entends tout ce que se fait dans nous de telle sorte que nous l'apercevons immiatement par nous-mes: c'est pourquoi non-seulement entendre, vouloir, imaginer, mais aussi sentir, c'est le chose ici que penser."--Principes de Philosophie. Ed. Cousin. 57.

"Toutes les proprique nous trouvons en la chose qui pense ne sont que des differentes de penser."--Ibid. 96.

[20] On the whole, it is pleasant to find satisfactory evidence that Hume knew nothing of the works of Spinoza; for the invariably abusive manner in which he refers to that type of the philosophic hero is only to be excused, if it is to be excused, by sheer ignorance of his life and work.

[21] For example, in discussing pride and humility, Hume says:--

"According as our idea of ourselves is more or less advantageous, we feel either of these opposite affections, and are elated by pride or dejected with humility ... when self enters not into the consideration there is no room either for pride or humility." That is, pride is pleasure, and humility is pain, associated with certain conceptions of one's self; or, as Spinoza puts it:-- "Superbia est de se pr?amore sui plus justo sentire" ("amor" being itia concomitante idea caus?extern?); and "Humilitas est tristitia orta ex eo quod homo suam impotentiam sive imbecillitatem contemplatur."

CHAPTER III.

THE ORIGIN OF THE IMPRESSIONS.

Admitting that the sensations, the feelings of pleasure and pain, and those of relation, are the primary irresolvable states of consciousness, two further lines of investigation present themselves. The one leads us to seek the origin of these "impressions;" the other, to inquire into the nature of the steps by which they become metamorphosed into those compound states of consciousness, which so largely enter into our ordinary trains of thought.

With respect to the origin of impressions of sensation, Hume is not quite consistent with himself. In one place (I. p. 117) he says, that it is impossible to decide "whether they arise immediately from the object, or are produced by the creative power of the mind, or are derived from the Author of our being," thereby implying that realism and idealism are equally probable hypotheses. But, in fact, after the demonstration by Descartes, that the immediate antecedents of sensations are changes in the nervous system, with which our feelings have no sort of resemblance, the hypothesis that sensations "arise immediately from the object" was out of court; and that Hume fully admitted the Cartesian doctrine is apparent when he says (I. p. 272):--

"All our perceptions are dependent on our organs and the disposition of our nerves and animal spirits."

And again, though in relation to another question, he observes:--

"There are three different kinds of impressions conveyed by the senses. The first are those of the figure, bulk, motion, and solidity of bodies. The second those of colours, tastes, smells, sounds, heat, and cold. The third are the pains and pleasures that arise from the application of objects to our bodies, as by the cutting of our flesh with steel, and such like. Both philosophers and the vulgar suppose the first of these to have a distinct continued existence. The vulgar only regard the second as on the same footing. Both philosophers and the vulgar again esteem the third to be merely perceptions, and consequently interrupted and dependent beings.

"Now 'tis evident that, whatever may be our philosophical opinion, colour, sounds, heat, and cold, as far as appears to the senses, exist after the same manner with motion and solidity; and that the difference we make between them, in this respect, arises not from the mere perception. So strong is the prejudice for the distinct continued existence of the former qualities, that when the contrary opinion is advanced by modern philosophers, people imagine they can almost refute it from their reason and experience, and that their very senses contradict this philosophy. 'Tis also evident that colours, sounds, &c., are originally on the same footing with the pain that arises from steel, and pleasure that proceeds from a fire; and that the difference betwixt them is founded neither on perception nor reason, but on the imagination. For as they are confessed to be, both of them, nothing but perceptions arising from the particular configurations and motions of the parts of body, wherein possibly can their difference consist? Upon the whole, then, we may conclude that, as far as the senses are judges, all perceptions are the same in the manner of their existence."--(I. p. 250, 251.)

The last words of this passage are as much Berkeley's as Hume's. But, instead of following Berkeley in his deductions from the position thus laid down, Hume, as the preceding citation shows, fully adopted the conclusion to which all that we know of psychological physiology tends, that the origin of the elements of consciousness, no less than that of all its other states, is to be sought in bodily changes, the seat of which can only be placed in the brain. And, as Locke had already done with less effect, he states and refutes the arguments commonly brought against the possibility of a causal connexion between the modes of motion of the cerebral substance and states of consciousness, with great clearness:--

"From these hypotheses concerning the substance and local conjunction of our perceptions we may pass to another, which is more intelligible than the former, and more important than the latter, viz. concerning the cause of our perceptions. Matter and motion, 'tis commonly said in the schools, however varied, are still matter and motion, and produce only a difference in the position and situation of objects. Divide a body as often as you please, 'tis still body. Place it in any figure, nothing ever results but figure, or the relation of parts. Move it in any manner, you still find motion or a change of relation. 'Tis absurd to imagine that motion in a circle, for instance, should be nothing but merely motion in a circle; while motion in another direction, as in an ellipse, should also be a passion or moral reflection; that the shocking of two globular particles should become a sensation of pain, and that the meeting of the triangular ones should afford a pleasure. Now as these different shocks and variations and mixtures are the only changes of which matter is susceptible, and as these never afford us any idea of thought or perception, 'tis concluded to be impossible, that thought can ever be caused by matter.

"Few have been able to withstand the seeming evidence of this argument; and yet nothing in the world is more easy than to refute it. We need only reflect upon what has been proved at large, that we are never sensible of any connexion between causes and effects, and that 'tis only by our experience of their constant conjunction we can arrive at any knowledge of this relation. Now, as all objects which are not contrary are susceptible of a constant conjunction, and as no real objects are contrary, I have inferred from these principles (Part III. ?15) that, to consider the matter a priori, anything may produce anything, and that we shall never discover a reason why any object may or may not be the cause of any other, however great, or however little, the resemblance may be betwixt them. This evidently destroys the precedent reasoning, concerning the cause of thought or perception. For though there appear no manner of connection betwixt motion and thought, the case is the same with all other causes and effects. Place one body of a pound weight on one end of a lever, and another body of the same weight on the other end; you will never find in these bodies any principle of motion dependent on their distance from the centre, more than of thought and perception. If you pretend, therefore, to prove, a priori, that such a position of bodies can never cause thought, because, turn it which way you will, it is nothing but a position of bodies: you must, by the same course of reasoning, conclude that it can never produce motion, since there is no more apparent connection in the one than in the other. But, as this latter conclusion is contrary to evident experience, and as 'tis possible we may have a like experience in the operations of the mind, and may perceive a constant conjunction of thought and motion, you reason too hastily when, from the mere consideration of the ideas, you conclude that 'tis impossible motion can ever produce thought, or a different position of parts give rise to a different passion or reflection. Nay, 'tis not only possible we may have such an experience, but 'tis certain we have it; since every one may perceive that the different dispositions of his body change his thoughts and sentiments. And should it be said that this depends on the union of soul and body, I would answer, that we must separate the question concerning the substance of the mind from that concerning the cause of its thought; and that, confining ourselves to the latter question, we find, by the comparing their ideas, that thought and motion are different from each other and by experience, that they are constantly united; which, being all the circumstances that enter into the idea of cause and effect, when applied to the operations of matter, we may certainly conclude that motion may be, and actually is, the cause of thought and perception."--(I. pp. 314-316.)

The upshot of all this is, that the "collection of perceptions," which constitutes the mind, is really a system of effects, the causes of which are to be sought in antecedent changes of the matter of the brain, just as the "collection of motions," which we call flying, is a system of effects, the causes of which are to be sought in the modes of motion of the matter of the muscles of the wings.

Hume, however, treats of this important topic only incidentally. He seems to have had very little acquaintance even with such physiology as was current in his time. At least, the only passage of his works, bearing on this subject, with which I am acquainted, contains nothing but a very odd version of the physiological views of Descartes:--

"When I received the relations of resemblance, contiguity, and causation, as principles of union among ideas, without examining into their causes, 'twas more in prosecution of my first maxim, that we must in the end rest contented with experience, than for want of something specious and plausible which I might have displayed on that subject. 'Twould have been easy to have made an imaginary dissection of the brain, and have shown why, upon our conception of any idea, the animal spirits run into all the contiguous traces and rouse up the other ideas that are related to it. But though I have neglected any advantage which I might have drawn from this topic in explaining the relations of ideas, I am afraid I must here have recourse to it, in order to account for the mistakes that arise from these relations. I shall therefore observe, that as the mind is endowed with the power of exciting any idea it pleases; whenever it despatches the spirits into that region of the brain in which the idea is placed; these spirits always excite the idea, when they run precisely into the proper traces and rummage that cell which belongs to the idea. But as their motion is seldom direct, and naturally turns a little to the one side or to the other; for this reason the animal spirits, falling into the contiguous traces, present other related ideas, in lieu of that which the mind desired at first to survey. This change we are not always sensible of; but continuing still the same train of thought, make use of the related idea which is presented to us and employ it in our reasonings, as if it were the same with what we demanded. This is the cause of many mistakes and sophisms in philosophy; as will naturally be imagined, and as it would be easy to show, if there was occasion."--(I. p. 88.)

Perhaps it is as well for Hume's fame that the occasion for further physiological speculations of this sort did not arise. But, while admitting the crudity of his notions and the strangeness of the language in which they are couched, it must in justice be remembered, that what are now known as the elements of the physiology of the nervous system were hardly dreamed of in the first half of the eighteenth century; and, as a further set off to Hume's credit, it must be noted that he grasped the fundamental truth, that the key to the comprehension of mental operations lies in the study of the molecular changes of the nervous apparatus by which they are originated.

Surely no one who is cognisant of the facts of the case, nowadays, doubts that the roots of psychology lie in the physiology of the nervous system. What we call the operations of the mind are functions of the brain, and the materials of consciousness are products of cerebral activity. Cabanis may have made use of crude and misleading phraseology when he said that the brain secretes thought as the liver secretes bile; but the conception which that much-abused phrase embodies is, nevertheless, far more consistent with fact than the popular notion that the mind is a metaphysical entity seated in the head, but as independent of the brain as a telegraph operator is of his instrument.

It is hardly necessary to point out that the doctrine just laid down is what is commonly called materialism. In fact, I am not sure that the adjective "crass," which appears to have a special charm for rhetorical sciolists, would not be applied to it. But it is, nevertheless, true that the doctrine contains nothing inconsistent with the purest idealism. For, as Hume remarks (as indeed Descartes had observed long before):--

"'Tis not our body we perceive when we regard our limbs and members, but certain impressions which enter by the senses; so that the ascribing a real and corporeal existence to these impressions, or to their objects, is an act of the mind as difficult to explain as that [the external existence of objects] which we examine at present."--(I. p. 249.)

Therefore, if we analyse the proposition that all mental phenomena are the effects or products of material phenomena, all that it means amounts to this; that whenever those states of consciousness which we call sensation, or emotion, or thought, come into existence, complete investigation will show good reason for the belief that they are preceded by those other phenomena of consciousness to which we give the names of matter and motion. All material changes appear, in the long run, to be modes of motion; but our knowledge of motion is nothing but that of a change in the place and order of our sensations; just as our knowledge of matter is restricted to those feelings of which we assume it to be the cause.

It has already been pointed out, that Hume must have admitted, and in fact does admit, the possibility that the mind is a Leibnitzian monad, or a Fichtean world-generating Ego, the universe of things being merely the picture produced by the evolution of the phenomena of consciousness. For any demonstration that can be given to the contrary effect, the "collection of perceptions" which makes up our consciousness may be an orderly phantasmagoria generated by the Ego, unfolding its successive scenes on the background of the abyss of nothingness; as a firework, which is but cunningly arranged combustibles, grows from a spark into a coruscation, and from a coruscation into figures, and words, and cascades of devouring fire, and then vanishes into the darkness of the night.

On the other hand, it must no less readily be allowed that, for anything that can be proved to the contrary, there may be a real something which is the cause of all our impressions; that sensations, though not likenesses, are symbols of that something; and that the part of that something, which we call the nervous system, is an apparatus for supplying us with a sort of algebra of fact, based on those symbols. A brain may be the machinery by which the material universe becomes conscious of itself. But it is important to notice that, even if this conception of the universe and of the relation of consciousness to its other components should be true, we should, nevertheless, be still bound by the limits of thought, still unable to refute the arguments of pure idealism. The more completely the materialistic position is admitted, the easier is it to show that the idealistic position is unassailable, if the idealist confines himself within the limits of positive knowledge.

Hume deals with the questions whether all our ideas are derived from experience, or whether, on the contrary, more or fewer of them are innate, which so much exercised the mind of Locke, after a somewhat summary fashion, in a note to the second section of the Inquiry:--

"It is probable that no more was meant by those who denied innate ideas, than that all ideas were copies of our impressions; though it must be confessed that the terms which they employed were not chosen with such caution, nor so exactly defined, as to prevent all mistakes about their doctrine. For what is meant by innate? If innate be equivalent to natural, then all the perceptions and ideas of the mind must be allowed to be innate or natural, in whatever sense we take the latter word, whether in opposition to what is uncommon, artificial, or miraculous. If by innate be meant contemporary with our birth, the dispute seems to be frivolous; nor is it worth while to inquire at what time thinking begins, whether before, at, or after our birth. Again, the word idea seems to be commonly taken in a very loose sense by Locke and others, as standing for any of our perceptions, our sensations and passions, as well as thoughts. Now in this sense I should desire to know what can be meant by asserting that self-love, or resentment of injuries, or the passion between the sexes is not innate?

"But admitting these terms, impressions and ideas, in the sense above explained, and understanding by innate what is original or copied from no precedent perception, then we may assert that all our impressions are innate, and our ideas not innate."

It would seem that Hume did not think it worth while to acquire a comprehension of the real points at issue in the controversy which he thus carelessly dismisses.

Yet Descartes has defined what he means by innate ideas with so much precision, that misconception ought to have been impossible. He says that, when he speaks of an idea being "innate," he means that it exists potentially in the mind, before it is actually called into existence by whatever is its appropriate exciting cause.

"I have never either thought or said," he writes, "that the mind has any need of innate ideas which are anything distinct from its faculty of thinking. But it is true that observing that there are certain thoughts which arise neither from external objects nor from the determination of my will, but only from my faculty of thinking; in order to mark the difference between the ideas or the notions which are the forms of these thoughts, and to distinguish them from the others, which may be called extraneous or voluntary, I have called them innate. But I have used this term in the same sense as when we say that generosity is innate in certain families; or that certain maladies, such as gout or gravel, are innate in others; not that children born in these families are troubled with such diseases in their mother's womb; but because they are born with the disposition or the faculty of contracting them."[22]

His troublesome disciple, Regius, having asserted that all our ideas come from observation or tradition, Descartes remarks:--

"So thoroughly erroneous is this assertion, that whoever has a proper comprehension of the action of our senses, and understands precisely the nature of that which is transmitted by them to our thinking faculty, will rather affirm that no ideas of things, such as are formed in thought, are brought to us by the senses, so that there is nothing in our ideas which is other than innate in the mind (naturel ?l'esprit), or in the faculty of thinking, if only certain circumstances are excepted, which belong only to experience. For example, it is experience alone which causes us to judge that such and such ideas, now present in our minds, are related to certain things which are external to us; not in truth, that they have been sent into our mind by these things, such as they are, by the organs of the senses; but because these organs have transmitted something which has occasioned the mind, in virtue of its innate power, to form them at this time rather than at another....

"Nothing passes from external objects to the soul except certain motions of matter (mouvemens corporels), but neither these motions, nor the figures which they produce, are conceived by us as they exist in the sensory organs, as I have fully explained in my "Dioptrics"; whence it follows that even the ideas of motion and of figures are innate (naturellement en nous). And, ?fortiori, the ideas of pain, of colours, of sounds, and of all similar things must be innate, in order that the mind may represent them to itself, on the occasion of certain motions of matter with which they have no resemblance."

Whoever denies what is, in fact, an inconceivable proposition, that sensations pass, as such, from the external world into the mind, must admit the conclusion here laid down by Descartes, that, strictly speaking, sensations, and ?fortiori, all the other contents of the mind, are innate. Or, to state the matter in accordance with the views previously expounded, that they are products of the inherent properties of the thinking organ, in which they lie potentially, before they are called into existence by their appropriate causes.

But if all the contents of the mind are innate, what is meant by experience?

It is the conversion, by unknown causes, of these innate potentialities into actual existences. The organ of thought, prior to experience, may be compared to an untouched piano, in which it may be properly said that music is innate, inasmuch as its mechanism contains, potentially, so many octaves of musical notes. The unknown cause of sensation which Descartes calls the "je ne sais quoi dans les objets" or "choses telles qu'elles sont," and Kant the "Noumenon" or "Ding an sich," is represented by the musician; who, by touching the keys, converts the potentiality of the mechanism into actual sounds. A note so produced is the equivalent of a single experience.

All the melodies and harmonies that proceed from the piano depend upon the action of the musician upon the keys. There is no internal mechanism which, when certain keys are struck, gives rise to an accompaniment of which the musician is only indirectly the cause. According to Descartes, however-- and this is what is generally fixed upon as the essence of his doctrine of innate ideas--the mind possesses such an internal mechanism, by which certain classes of thoughts are generated, on the occasion of certain experiences. Such thoughts are innate, just as sensations are innate; they are not copies of sensations, any more than sensations are copies of motions; they are invariably generated in the mind, when certain experiences arise in it, just as sensations are invariably generated when certain bodily motions take place; they are universal, inasmuch as they arise under the same conditions in all men; they are necessary, because their genesis under these conditions is invariable. These innate thoughts are what Descartes terms truths: that is beliefs--and his notions respecting them are plainly set forth in a passage of the Principes.

"Thus far I have discussed that which we know as things: it remains that I should speak of that which we know as truths. For example, when we think that it is impossible to make anything out of nothing, we do not imagine that this proposition is a thing which exists, or a property of something, but we take it for a certain eternal truth, which has its seat in the mind, and is called a common notion or an axiom. Similarly, when we affirm that it is impossible that one and the same thing should exist and not exist at the same time; that

that which has been created should not have been created; that he who thinks must exist while he thinks; and a number of other like propositions; these are only truths, and not things which exist outside our thoughts. And there is such a number of these that it would be wearisome to enumerate them: nor is it necessary to do so, because we cannot fail to know them when the occasion of thinking about them presents itself, and we are not blinded by any prejudices."

It would appear that Locke was not more familiar with Descartes' writings than Hume seems to have been; for, viewed in relation to the passages just cited, the arguments adduced in his famous polemic against innate ideas are totally irrelevant.

It has been shown that Hume practically, if not in so many words, admits the justice of Descartes' assertion that, strictly speaking, sensations are innate; that is to say, that they are the product of the reaction of the organ of the mind on the stimulus of an "unknown cause," which is Descartes' "je ne sais quoi." Therefore, the difference between Descartes' opinion and that of Hume resolves itself into this: Given sensation-experiences, can all the contents of consciousness be derived from the collocation and metamorphosis of these experiences? Or, are new elements of consciousness, products of an innate potentiality distinct from sensibility, added to these? Hume affirms the former position, Descartes the latter. If the analysis of the phenomena of consciousness given in the preceding pages is correct, Hume is in error; while the father of modern philosophy had a truer insight, though he overstated the case. For want of sufficiently searching psychological investigations, Descartes was led to suppose that innumerable ideas, the evolution of which in the course of experience can be demonstrated, were direct or innate products of the thinking faculty.

As has been already pointed out, it is the great merit of Kant that he started afresh on the track indicated by Descartes, and steadily upheld the doctrine of the existence of elements of consciousness, which are neither sense-experiences nor any modifications of them. We may demur to the expression that space and time are forms of sensory intuition; but it imperfectly represents the great fact that co-existence and succession are mental phenomena not given in the mere sense experience.[23]

FOOTNOTES:

[22] Remarques de Ren?Descartes sur un certain placard imprim?aux Pays Bas vers la fin de l'ann, 1647.--Descartes, OEuvres. Ed. Cousin, x. p. 71.

[23] "Wir knen uns keinen Gegenstand denken, ohne durch Kategorien; nen keinen gedachten Gegenstand erkennen, ohne durch Anschauungen, die jenen Begriffen entsprechen. Nun sind alle unsere Anschauungen sinnlich, und diese Erkenntniss, so fern der Gegenstand derselben gegeben ist, ist empirisch. Empirische Erkenntniss aber ist Erfahrung. Folglich ist uns keine Erkenntniss."

"Aber diese Erkenntniss, die bloss auf Gegenst 鋘 de der Erfahrung eingeschrekt ist, ist darum nicht alle von der Erfahrung entlehnt, sondern was sowohl die reinen Anschauungen, als die reinen Verstandesbegriffe betrifft, so sind sie Elemente der Erkenntniss die in uns a priori angetroffen werden."--Kritik der reinen Vernunft. Elementarlehre, p. 135.

Without a glossary explanatory of Kant's terminology, this passage would be hardly intelligible in a translation; but it may be paraphrased thus: All knowledge is founded upon experiences of sensation, but it is not all derived from those experiences; inasmuch as the impressions of relation ("reine Anschauungen"; "reine Verstandesbegriffe") have a potential or ?priori existence in us, and by their addition to sense-experiences, constitute knowledge.

CHAPTER IV.

THE CLASSIFICATION AND THE NOMENCLATURE OF MENTAL OPERATIONS.

If, as has been set forth in the preceding chapter, all mental states are effects of physical causes, it follows that what are called mental faculties and operations are, properly speaking, cerebral functions, allotted to definite, though not yet precisely assignable, parts of the brain.

These functions appear to be reducible to three groups, namely: Sensation, Correlation, and Ideation.

The organs of the functions of sensation and correlation are those portions of the cerebral substance, the molecular changes of which give rise to impressions of sensation and impressions of relation.

The changes in the nervous matter which bring about the effects which we call its functions, follow upon some kind of stimulus, and rapidly reaching their maximum, as rapidly die away. The effect of the irritation of a nerve-fibre on the cerebral substance with which it is connected may be compared to the pulling of a long bell-wire. The impulse takes a little time to reach the bell; the bell rings and then becomes quiescent, until another pull is given. So, in the brain, every sensation is the ring of a cerebral particle, the effect of a momentary impulse sent along a nerve-fibre.

If there were a complete likeness between the two terms of this very rough and ready comparison, it is obvious that there could be no such thing as memory. A bell records no audible sign of having been rung five minutes ago, and the activity of a sensigenous cerebral particle might similarly leave no trace. Under these circumstances, again, it would seem that the only impressions of relation which could arise would be those of co-existence and of similarity. For succession implies memory of an antecedent state.[24]

But the special peculiarity of the cerebral apparatus is, that any given function which has once been performed is very easily set a-going again, by causes more or less different from those to which it owed its origin. Of the mechanism of this generation of images of impressions or ideas (in Hume's sense), which may be termed Ideation, we know nothing at present, though the fact and its results are familiar enough.

During our waking, and many of our sleeping, hours, in fact, the function of ideation is in continual, if not continuous, activity. Trains of thought, as we call them, succeed one another without intermission, even when the starting of new trains by fresh sense-impressions is as far as possible prevented. The rapidity and the intensity of this ideational process are obviously dependent upon physiological conditions. The widest differences in these respects are constitutional in men of different temperaments; and are observable in oneself, under varying conditions of hunger and repletion, fatigue and freshness, calmness and emotional excitement. The influence of diet on dreams; of stimulants upon the fulness and the velocity of the stream of thought; the delirious phantasms generated by disease, by hashish, or by alcohol; will occur to every one as examples of the marvellous sensitiveness of the apparatus of ideation to purely physical influences.

The succession of mental states in ideation is not fortuitous, but follows the law of association, which may be stated thus: that every idea tends to be followed by some other idea which is associated with the first, or its impression, by a relation of succession, of contiguity, or of likeness.

Thus the idea of the word horse just now presented itself to my mind, and was followed in quick succession by the ideas of four legs, hoofs, teeth, rider, saddle, racing, cheating; all of which ideas are connected in my experience with the impression, or the idea, of a horse and with one another, by the relations of contiguity and succession. No great attention to what passes in the mind is needful to prove that our trains of thought are neither to be arrested, nor even permanently controlled, by our desires or emotions. Nevertheless they are largely influenced by them. In the presence of a strong desire, or emotion, the stream of thought no longer flows on in a straight course, but seems, as it were, to eddy round the idea of that which is the object of the emotion. Every one who has "eaten his bread in sorrow" knows how strangely the current of ideas whirls about the conception of the object of regret or remorse as a centre; every now and then, indeed, breaking away into the new tracks suggested by passing associations, but still returning to the central thought. Few can have been so happy as to have escaped the social bore, whose pet notion is certain to crop up whatever topic is started; while the fixed idea of the monomaniac is but the extreme form of the same phenomenon.

And as, on the one hand, it is so hard to drive away the thought we would fain be rid of; so, upon the other, the pleasant imaginations which we would so gladly retain are, sooner or later, jostled away by the crowd of claimants for birth into the world of consciousness; which hover as a sort of psychical possibilities, or inverse ghosts, the bodily presentments of spiritual phenomena to be, in the limbo of the brain. In that form of desire which is called "attention," the train of thought, held fast, for a time, in the desired direction, seems ever striving to get on to another line--and the junctions and sidings are so multitudinous!

The constituents of trains of ideas may be grouped in various ways.

Hume says:--

"We find, by experience, that when any impression has been present in the mind, it again makes its appearance there as an idea, and this it may do in two different ways: either when, on its new appearance, it retains a considerable degree of its first vivacity, and is somewhat intermediate between an impression and an idea; or when it entirely loses that vivacity, and is a perfect idea. The faculty by which we repeat our impressions in the first manner, is called the memory, and the other the imagination."--(I. pp. 23, 24.)

And he considers that the only difference between ideas of imagination and those of memory, except the superior vivacity of the latter, lies in the fact that those of memory preserve the original order of the impressions from which they are derived, while the imagination "is free to transpose and change its ideas."

The latter statement of the difference between memory and imagination is less open to cavil than the former, though by no means unassailable.

The special characteristic of a memory surely is not its vividness; but that it is a complex idea, in which the idea of that which is remembered is related by co-existence with other ideas, and by antecedence with present impressions.

If I say I remember A. B., the chance acquaintance of ten years ago, it is not because my idea of A. B. is very vivid--on the contrary, it is extremely faint-- but because that idea is associated with ideas of impressions co-existent with those which I call A. B.; and that all these are at the end of the long series of ideas, which represent that much past time. In truth I have a much more vivid idea of Mr. Pickwick, or of Colonel Newcome, than I have of A. B.; but, associated with the ideas of these persons, I have no idea of their having ever been derived from the world of impressions; and so they are relegated to the world of imagination. On the other hand, the characteristic of an imagination may properly be said to lie not in its intensity, but in the fact that, as Hume puts it, "the arrangement," or the relations, of the ideas are different from those in which the impressions, whence these ideas are derived, occurred; or in other words, that the thing imagined has not happened. In popular usage, however, imagination is frequently employed for simple memory--"In imagination I was back in the old times."

It is a curious omission on Hume's part that, while thus dwelling on two classes of ideas, Memories and Imaginations, he has not, at the same time, taken notice of a third group, of no small importance, which are as different from imaginations as memories are; though, like the latter, they are often confounded with pure imaginations in general speech. These are the ideas of expectation, or as they may be called for the sake of brevity, Expectations; which differ from simple imaginations in being associated with the idea of the existence of corresponding impressions, in the future, just as memories contain the idea of the existence of the corresponding impressions in the past.

The ideas belonging to two of the three groups enumerated: namely, memories and expectations, present some features, of particular interest. And first, with respect to memories.

In Hume's words, all simple ideas are copies of simple impressions. The idea of a single sensation is a faint, but accurate, image of that sensation; the idea of a relation is a reproduction of the feeling of co-existence, of succession, or of similarity. But, when complex impressions or complex ideas are reproduced as memories, it is probable that the copies never give all the details of the originals with perfect accuracy, and it is certain that they rarely do so. No one possesses a memory so good, that if he has only once observed a natural object, a second inspection does not show him something that he has forgotten. Almost all, if not all, our memories are therefore sketches, rather than portraits, of the originals--the salient features are obvious, while the subordinate characters are obscure or unrepresented.

Now, when several complex impressions which are more or less different from one another--let us say that out of ten impressions in each, six are the same in all, and four are different from all the rest--are successively presented to the mind, it is easy to see what must be the nature of the result. The repetition of the six similar impressions will strengthen the six corresponding elements of the complex idea, which will therefore acquire greater vividness; while the four differing impressions of each will not only acquire no greater strength than they had at first, but, in accordance with the law of association, they will all tend to appear at once, and will thus neutralise one another.

This mental operation may be rendered comprehensible by considering what takes place in the formation of compound photographs--when the images of the faces of six sitters, for example, are each received on the same photographic plate, for a sixth of the time requisite to take one portrait. The final result is that all those points in which the six faces agree are brought out strongly, while all those in which they differ are left vague; and thus what may be termed a generic portrait of the six, in contradistinction to a specific portrait of any one, is produced.

Thus our ideas of single complex impressions are incomplete in one way, and those of numerous, more or less similar, complex impressions are incomplete in another way; that is to say, they are generic, not specific. And hence it follows, that our ideas of the impressions in question are not, in the strict sense of the word, copies of those impressions; while, at the same time, they may exist in the mind independently of language.

The generic ideas which are formed from several similar, but not identical, complex experiences are what are commonly called abstract or general ideas; and Berkeley endeavoured to prove that all general ideas are nothing but particular ideas annexed to a certain term, which gives them a more extensive signification, and makes them recall, upon occasion, other individuals which are similar to them. Hume says that he regards this as "one of the greatest and the most valuable discoveries that has been made of late years in the republic of letters," and endeavours to confirm it in such a manner that it shall be "put beyond all doubt and controversy."

I may venture to express a doubt whether he has succeeded in his object; but the subject is an abstruse one; and I must content myself with the remark, that though Berkeley's view appears to be largely applicable to such general ideas as are formed after language has been acquired, and to all the more abstract sort of conceptions, yet that general ideas of sensible objects may nevertheless be produced in the way indicated, and may exist independently of language. In dreams, one sees houses, trees and other objects, which are perfectly recognisable as such, but which remind one of the actual objects as seen "out of the corner of the eye," or of the pictures thrown by a badlyfocussed magic lantern. A man addresses us who is like a figure seen by twilight; or we travel through countries where every feature of the scenery is vague; the outlines of the hills are ill-marked, and the rivers have no defined banks. They are, in short, generic ideas of many past impressions of men, hills, and rivers. An anatomist who occupies himself intently with the examination of several specimens of some new kind of animal, in course of time acquires so vivid a conception of its form and structure, that the idea may take visible shape and become a sort of waking dream. But the figure which thus presents itself is generic, not specific. It is no copy of any one specimen, but, more or less, a mean of the series; and there seems no reason to doubt that the minds of children before they learn to speak, and of deaf mutes, are peopled with similarly generated generic ideas of sensible objects.

It has been seen that a memory is a complex idea made up of at least two constituents. In the first place there is the idea of an object; and secondly, there is the idea of the relation of antecedence between that object and some present objects.

To say that one has a recollection of a given event and to express the belief that it happened, are two ways of giving an account of one and the same mental fact. But the former mode of stating the fact of memory is preferable, at present, because it certainly does not presuppose the existence of language in the mind of the rememberer; while it may be said that the latter does. It is perfectly possible to have the idea of an event A, and of the events B, C, D, which came between it and the present state E, as mere mental pictures. It is hardly to be doubted that children have very distinct memories long before they can speak; and we believe that such is the case because they act upon their memories. But, if they act upon their memories, they to all intents and purposes believe their memories. In other words, though, being devoid of language, the child cannot frame a proposition expressive of belief; cannot say "sugar-plum was sweet;" yet the psychical operation of which that proposition is merely the verbal expression, is perfectly effected. The experience of the co-existence of sweetness with sugar has produced a state of mind which bears the same relation to a verbal proposition, as the natural disposition to produce a given idea, assumed to exist by Descartes as an "innate idea" would bear to that idea put into words.

The fact that the beliefs of memory precede the use of language, and therefore are originally purely instinctive, and independent of any rational justification, should have been of great importance to Hume, from its bearing upon his theory of causation; and it is curious that he has not adverted to it, but always takes the trustworthiness of memories for granted. It may be worth while briefly to make good the omission.

That I was in pain, yesterday, is as certain to me as any matter of fact can be; by no effort of the imagination is it possible for me really to entertain the contrary belief. At the same time, I am bound to admit, that the whole foundation for my belief is the fact, that the idea of pain is indissolubly associated in my mind with the idea of that much past time. Any one who will be at the trouble may provide himself with hundreds of examples to the same effect.

This and similar observations are important under another aspect. They prove that the idea of even a single strong impression may be so powerfully associated with that of a certain time, as to originate a belief of which the contrary is inconceivable, and which may therefore be properly said to be necessary. A single weak, or moderately strong, impression may not be represented by any memory. But this defect of weak experiences may be compensated by their repetition; and what Hume means by "custom" or "habit" is simply the repetition of experiences.

"wherever the repetition of any particular act or operation produces a propensity to renew the same act or operation, without being impelled by any reasoning or process of the understanding, we always say that this propensity is the effect of Custom. By employing that word, we pretend not to have given the ultimate reason of such a propensity. We only point out a principle of human nature which is universally acknowledged, and which is well known by its effects."--(IV. p. 52.)

It has been shown that an expectation is a complex idea which, like a memory, is made up of two constituents. The one is the idea of an object, the other is the idea of a relation of sequence between that object and some present object; and the reasoning which applied to memories applies to expectations. To have an expectation[25] of a given event, and to believe that it will happen, are only two modes of stating the same fact. Again, just in the same way as we call a memory, put into words, a belief, so we give the same name to an expectation in like clothing. And the fact already cited, that a child before it can speak acts upon its memories, is good evidence that it forms expectations. The infant who knows the meaning neither of "sugar-plum" nor of "sweet," nevertheless is in full possession of that complex idea, which, when he has learned to employ language, will take the form of the verbal proposition, "A sugar-plum will be sweet."

 Thus, beliefs of expectation, or at any rate their potentialities, are, as much as those of memory, antecedent to speech, and are as incapable of justification by any logical process. In fact, expectations are but memories inverted. The association which is the foundation of expectation must exist as a memory before it can play its part. As Hume says,--

 " ... it is certain we here advance a very intelligible proposition at least, if not a true one, when we assert that after the constant conjunction of two objects, heat and flame, for instance, weight and solidity, we are determined by custom alone to expect the one from the appearance of the other. This hypothesis seems even the only one which explains the difficulty why we draw from a thousand instances, an inference which we are not able to draw from one instance, that is in no respect different from them."...

 "Custom, then, is the great guide of human life. It is that principle alone which renders our experience useful to us, and makes us expect, for the future, a similar train of events with those which have appeared in the past."...

 "All belief of matter-of-fact or real existence is derived merely from some object present to the memory or senses, and a customary conjunction between that and some other object; or in other words, having found, in many instances, that any two kinds of objects, flame and heat, snow and cold, have always been conjoined together: if flame or snow be presented anew to the senses, the mind is carried by custom to expect heat or cold, and to believe that such a quality does exist, and will discover itself upon a nearer approach. This belief is the necessary result of placing the mind in such circumstances. It is an operation of the soul, when we are so situated, as unavoidable as to feel the passion of love, when we receive benefits, or hatred, when we meet with injuries. All these operations are a species of natural instincts, which no reasoning or process of the thought and understanding is able either to produce or to prevent."--(IV. pp. 52-56.)

The only comment that appears needful here is, that Hume has attached somewhat too exclusive a weight to that repetition of experiences to which alone the term "custom" can be properly applied. The proverb says that "a burnt child dreads the fire"; and any one who will make the experiment will find, that one burning is quite sufficient to establish an indissoluble belief that contact with fire and pain go together.

As a sort of inverted memory, expectation follows the same laws; hence, while a belief of expectation is, in most cases, as Hume truly says, established by custom, or the repetition of weak impressions, it may quite well be based upon a single strong experience. In the absence of language, a specific memory cannot be strengthened by repetition. It is obvious that that which has happened cannot happen again, with the same collateral associations of co-existence and succession. But, memories of the co-existence and succession of impressions are capable of being indefinitely strengthened by the recurrence of similar impressions, in the same order, even though the collateral associations are totally different; in fact, the ideas of these impressions become generic.

If I recollect that a piece of ice was cold yesterday, nothing can strengthen the recollection of that particular fact; on the contrary, it may grow weaker, in the absence of any record of it. But if I touch ice to-day and again find it cold, the association is repeated, and the memory of it becomes stronger. And, by this very simple process of repetition of experience, it has become utterly impossible for us to think of having handled ice without thinking of its coldness. But, that which is, under the one aspect, the strengthening of a memory, is, under the other, the intensification of an expectation. Not only can we not think of having touched ice, without feeling cold, but we cannot think of touching ice, in the future, without expecting to feel cold. An expectation so strong that it cannot be changed, or abolished, may thus be generated out of repeated experiences. And it is important to note that such expectations may be formed quite unconsciously. In my dressing room, a certain can is usually kept full of water, and I am in the habit of lifting it to pour out water for washing. Sometimes the servant has forgotten to fill it, and then I find that, when I take hold of the handle, the can goes up with a jerk. Long association has, in fact, led me to expect the can to have a considerable weight; and, quite unawares, my muscular effort is adjusted to the expectation.

The process of strengthening generic memories of succession, and, at the same time, intensifying expectations of succession, is what is commonly called verification. The impression B has frequently been observed to follow the impression A. The association thus produced is represented as the memory, A -> B. When the impression A appears again, the idea of B follows, associated with that of the immediate appearance of the impression B. If the impression B does appear, the expectation is said to be verified; while the memory A -> B is strengthened, and gives rise in turn to a stronger expectation. And repeated verification may render that expectation so strong that its non-verification is inconceivable.

FOOTNOTES:

[24] It is not worth while, for the present purpose, to consider whether, as all nervous action occupies a sensible time, the duration of one impression might not overlap that of the impression which follows it, in the case supposed.

[25] We give no name to faint memories; but expectations of like character play so large a part in human affairs that they, together with the associated emotions of pleasure and pain, are distinguished as "hopes" or "fears."

CHAPTER V.

THE MENTAL PHENOMENA OF ANIMALS.

In the course of the preceding chapters, attention has been more than once called to the fact, that the elements of consciousness and the operations of the mental faculties, under discussion, exist independently of and antecedent to, the existence of language.

If any weight is to be attached to arguments from analogy, there is overwhelming evidence in favour of the belief that children, before they can speak, and deaf mutes, possess the feelings to which those who have acquired the faculty of speech apply the name of sensations; that they have the feelings of relation; that trains of ideas pass through their minds; that generic ideas are formed from specific ones; and, that among these, ideas of memory and expectation occupy a most important place, inasmuch as, in their quality of potential beliefs, they furnish the grounds of action. This conclusion, in truth, is one of those which, though they cannot be demonstrated, are never doubted; and, since it is highly probable and cannot be disproved, we are quite safe in accepting it, as, at any rate, a good working hypothesis.

But, if we accept it, we must extend it to a much wider assemblage of living beings. Whatever cogency is attached to the arguments in favour of the occurrence of all the fundamental phenomena of mind in young children and deaf mutes, an equal force must be allowed to appertain to those which may be adduced to prove that the higher animals have minds. We must admit that Hume does not express himself too strongly when he says--

"no truth appears to me more evident, than that the beasts are endowed with thought and reason as well as men. The arguments are in this case so obvious, that they never escape the most stupid and ignorant."--(I. p. 232.)

In fact, this is one of the few cases in which the conviction which forces itself upon the stupid and the ignorant, is fortified by the reasonings of the intelligent, and has its foundation deepened by every increase of knowledge. It is not merely that the observation of the actions of animals almost irresistibly suggests the attribution to them of mental states, such as those which accompany corresponding actions in men. The minute comparison which has been instituted by anatomists and physiologists between the organs which we know to constitute the apparatus of thought in man, and the corresponding organs in brutes, has demonstrated the existence of the closest similarity between the two, not only in structure, as far as the microscope will carry us, but in function, as far as functions are determinable by experiment. There is no question in the mind of any one acquainted with the facts that, so far as observation and experiment can take us, the structure and the functions of the nervous system are fundamentally the same in an ape, or in a dog, and in a man. And the suggestion that we must stop at the exact point at which direct proof fails us; and refuse to believe that the similarity which extends so far stretches yet further, is no better than a quibble. Robinson Crusoe did not feel bound to conclude, from the single human footprint which he saw in the sand, that the maker of the impression had only one leg.

Structure for structure, down to the minutest microscopical details, the eye, the ear, the olfactory organs, the nerves, the spinal cord, the brain of an ape, or of a dog, correspond with the same organs in the human subject. Cut a nerve, and the evidence of paralysis, or of insensibility, is the same in the two cases; apply pressure to the brain, or administer a narcotic, and the signs of intelligence disappear in the one as in the other. Whatever reason we have for believing that the changes which take place in the normal cerebral substance of man give rise to states of consciousness, the same reason exists for the belief that the modes of motion of the cerebral substance of an ape, or of a dog, produce like effects.

A dog acts as if he had all the different kinds of impressions of sensation of which each of us is cognisant. Moreover, he governs his movements exactly as if he had the feelings of distance, form, succession, likeness, and unlikeness, with which we are familiar, or as if the impressions of relation were generated in his mind as they are in our own. Sleeping dogs frequently appear to dream. If they do, it must be admitted that ideation goes on in them while they are asleep; and, in that case, there is no reason to doubt that they are conscious of trains of ideas in their waking state. Further, that dogs, if they possess ideas at all, have memories and expectations, and those potential beliefs of which these states are the foundation, can hardly be doubted by any one who is conversant with their ways. Finally, there would appear to be no valid argument against the supposition that dogs form generic ideas of sensible objects. One of the most curious peculiarities of the dog mind is its inherent snobbishness, shown by the regard paid to external respectability. The dog who barks furiously at a beggar will let a well-dressed man pass him without opposition. Has he not then a "generic idea" of rags and dirt associated with the idea of aversion, and that of sleek broadcloth associated with the idea of liking?

In short, it seems hard to assign any good reason for denying to the higher animals any mental state, or process, in which the employment of the vocal or visual symbols of which language is composed is not involved; and comparative psychology confirms the position in relation to the rest of the animal world assigned to man by comparative anatomy. As comparative anatomy is easily able to show that, physically, man is but the last term of a long series of forms, which lead, by slow gradations, from the highest mammal to the almost formless speck of living protoplasm, which lies on the shadowy boundary between animal and vegetable life; so, comparative psychology, though but a young science, and far short of her elder sister's growth, points to the same conclusion.

In the absence of a distinct nervous system, we have no right to look for its product, consciousness; and, even in those forms of animal life in which the nervous apparatus has reached no higher degree of development, than that exhibited by the system of the spinal cord and the foundation of the brain in ourselves, the argument from analogy leaves the assumption of the existence of any form of consciousness unsupported. With the super-addition of a nervous apparatus corresponding with the cerebrum in ourselves, it is allowable to suppose the appearance of the simplest states of consciousness, or the sensations; and it is conceivable that these may at first exist, without any power of reproducing them, as memories; and, consequently, without ideation. Still higher, an apparatus of correlation may be superadded, until, as all these organs become more developed, the condition of the highest speechless animals is attained.

It is a remarkable example of Hume's sagacity that he perceived the importance of a branch of science which, even now, can hardly be said to exist; and that, in a remarkable passage, he sketches in bold outlines the chief features of comparative psychology.

" ... any theory, by which we explain the operations of the understanding, or the origin and connexion of the passions in man, will acquire additional authority if we find that the same theory is requisite to explain the same phenomena in all other animals. We shall make trial of this with regard to the hypothesis by which we have, in the foregoing discourse, endeavoured to account for all experimental reasonings; and It Is hoped that this new point of view will serve to confirm all our former observations.

"First, it seems evident that animals, as well as men, learn many things from experience, and infer that the same events will always follow from the same causes. By this principle they become acquainted with the more obvious properties of external objects, and gradually, from their birth, treasure up a knowledge of the nature of fire, water, earth, stones, heights, depths, &c., and of the effects which result from their operation. The ignorance and inexperience of the young are here plainly distinguishable from the cunning and sagacity of the old, who have learned, by long observation, to avoid what hurt them, and pursue what gave ease or pleasure. A horse that has been accustomed to the field, becomes acquainted with the proper height which he can leap, and will never attempt what exceeds his force and ability. An old greyhound will trust the more fatiguing part of the chase to the younger, and will place himself so as to meet the hare in her doubles; nor are the conjectures which he forms on this occasion founded on anything but his observation and experience.

"This is still more evident from the effects of discipline and education on animals, who, by the proper application of rewards and punishments, may be taught any course of action, the most contrary to their natural instincts and propensities. Is it not experience which renders a dog apprehensive of pain when you menace him, or lift up the whip to beat him? Is it not even experience which makes him answer to his name, and infer from such an arbitrary sound that you mean him rather than any of his fellows, and intend to call him, when you pronounce it in a certain manner and with a certain tone and accent?

"In all these cases we may observe that the animal infers some fact beyond what immediately strikes his senses; and that this inference is altogether founded on past experience, while the creature expects from the present object the same consequences which it has always found in its observation to result from similar objects.

"Secondly, it is impossible that this inference of the animal can be founded on any process of argument or reasoning, by which he concludes that like events must follow like objects, and that the course of nature will always be regular in its operations. For if there be in reality any arguments of this nature they surely lie too abstruse for the observation of such imperfect understandings; since it may well employ the utmost care and attention of a philosophic genius to discover and observe them. Animals therefore are not guided in these inferences by reasoning; neither are children; neither are the generality of mankind in their ordinary actions and conclusions; neither are philosophers themselves, who, in all the active parts of life, are in the main the same as the vulgar, and are governed by the same maxims. Nature must have provided some other principle, of more ready and more general use and application; nor can an operation of such immense consequence in life as that of inferring effects from causes, be trusted to the uncertain process of reasoning and argumentation. Were this doubtful with regard to men, it seems to admit of no question with regard to the brute creation; and the conclusion being once firmly established in the one, we have a strong presumption, from all the rules of analogy, that it ought to be universally admitted, without any exception or reserve. It is custom alone which engages animals, from every object that strikes their senses, to infer its usual attendant, and carries their imagination from the appearance of the one to conceive the other, in that particular manner which we denominate belief. No other explication can be given of this operation in all the higher as well as lower classes of sensitive beings which fall under our notice and observation."--(IV. pp. 122-4.)

It will be observed that Hume appears to contrast the "inference of the animal" with the "process of argument or reasoning in man." But it would be a complete misapprehension of his intention, if we were to suppose, that he thereby means to imply that there is any real difference between the two processes. The "inference of the animal" is a potential belief of expectation; the process of argument, or reasoning, in man is based upon potential beliefs of expectation, which are formed in the man exactly in the same way as in the animal. But, in men endowed with speech, the mental state which constitutes the potential belief is represented by a verbal proposition, and thus becomes what all the world recognises as a belief. The fallacy which Hume combats is, that the proposition, or verbal representative of a belief, has come to be regarded as a reality, instead of as the mere symbol which it really is; and that reasoning, or logic, which deals with nothing but propositions, is supposed to be necessary in order to validate the natural fact symbolised by those propositions. It is a fallacy similar to that of supposing that money is the foundation of wealth, whereas it is only the wholly unessential symbol of property.

In the passage which immediately follows that just quoted, Hume makes admissions which might be turned to serious account against some of his own doctrines.

"But though animals learn many parts of their knowledge from observation, there are also many parts of it which they derive from the original hand of Nature, which much exceed the share of capacity they possess on ordinary occasions, and in which they improve, little or nothing, by the longest practice and experience. These we denominate INSTINCTS, and are so apt to admire as something very extraordinary and inexplicable by all the disquisitions of human understanding. But our wonder will perhaps cease or diminish when we consider that the experimental reasoning itself, which we possess in common with beasts, and on which the whole conduct of life depends, is nothing but a species of instinct or mechanical power, that acts in us unknown to ourselves, and in its chief operations is not directed by any such relations or comparison of ideas as are the proper objects of our intellectual faculties.

"Though the instinct be different, yet still it is an instinct which teaches a man to avoid the fire, as much as that which teaches a bird, with such exactness, the art of incubation and the whole economy and order of its nursery."--(IV. pp. 125, 126.)

The parallel here drawn between the "avoidance of a fire" by a man and the incubatory instinct of a bird is inexact. The man avoids fire when he has had experience of the pain produced by burning; but the bird incubates the first time it lays eggs, and therefore before it has had any experience of incubation. For the comparison to be admissible, it would be necessary that a man should avoid fire the first time he saw it, which is notoriously not the case.

The term "instinct" is very vague and ill-defined. It is commonly employed to denote any action, or even feeling, which is not dictated by conscious reasoning, whether it is, or is not, the result of previous experience. It is "instinct" which leads a chicken just hatched to pick up a grain of corn; parental love is said to be "instinctive"; the drowning man who catches at a straw does it "instinctively"; and the hand that accidentally touches something hot is drawn back by "instinct." Thus "instinct" is made to cover everything from a simple reflex movement, in which the organ of consciousness need not be at all implicated, up to a complex combination of acts directed towards a definite end and accompanied by intense consciousness.

But this loose employment of the term "instinct" really accords with the nature of the thing; for it is wholly impossible to draw any line of demarcation between reflex actions and instincts. If a frog, on the flank of which a little drop of acid has been placed, rubs it off with the foot of the same side; and, if that foot be held, performs the same operation, at the cost of much effort, with the other foot, it certainly displays a curious instinct. But it is no less true that the whole operation is a reflex operation of the spinal cord, which can be performed quite as well when the brain is destroyed; and between which and simple reflex actions there is a complete series of gradations. In like manner, when an infant takes the breast, it is impossible to say whether the action should be rather termed instinctive or reflex.

What are usually called the instincts of animals are, however, acts of such a nature that, if they were performed by men, they would involve the generation of a series of ideas and of inferences from them; and it is a curious, and apparently an insoluble, problem whether they are, or are not, accompanied by cerebral changes of the same nature as those which give rise to ideas and inferences in ourselves. When a chicken picks up a grain, for example, are there, firstly, certain sensations, accompanied by the feeling of relation between the grain and its own body; secondly, a desire of the grain; thirdly, a volition to seize it? Or, are only the sensational terms of the series actually represented in consciousness?

The latter seems the more probable opinion, though it must be admitted that the other alternative is possible. But, in this case, the series of mental states which occurs is such as would be represented in language by a series of propositions, and would afford proof positive of the existence of innate ideas, in the Cartesian sense. Indeed, a metaphysical fowl, brooding over the mental operations of his fully-fledged consciousness, might appeal to the fact as proof that, in the very first action of his life, he assumed the existence of the Ego and the non-Ego, and of a relation between the two.

In all seriousness, if the existence of instincts be granted, the possibility of the existence of innate ideas, in the most extended sense ever imagined by Descartes, must also be admitted. In fact, Descartes, as we have soon, illustrates what he means by an innate idea, by the analogy of hereditary diseases or hereditary mental peculiarities, such as generosity. On the other hand, hereditary mental tendencies may justly be termed instincts; and still more appropriately might those special proclivities, which constitute what we call genius, come into the same category.

The child who is impelled to draw as soon as it can hold a pencil; the Mozart who breaks out into music as early; the boy Bidder who worked out the most complicated sums without learning arithmetic; the boy Pascal who evolved Euclid out of his own consciousness: all these may be said to have been impelled by instinct, as much as are the beaver and the bee. And the man of genius, is distinct in kind from the man of cleverness, by reason of the working within him of strong innate tendencies--which cultivation may improve, but which it can no more create, than horticulture can make thistles bear figs. The analogy between a musical instrument and the mind holds good here also. Art and industry may get much music, of a sort, out of a penny whistle; but, when all is done, it has no chance against an organ. The innate musical potentialities of the two are infinitely different.

CHAPTER VI.

LANGUAGE--PROPOSITIONS CONCERNING NECESSARY TRUTHS.

Though we may accept Hume's conclusion that speechless animals think, believe, and reason; yet, it must be borne in mind, that there is an important difference between the signification of the terms when applied to them and when applied to those animals which possess language. The thoughts of the former are trains of mere feelings; those of the latter are, in addition, trains of the ideas of the signs which represent feelings, and which are called "words."

A word, in fact, is a spoken or written sign, the idea of which is, by repetition, so closely associated with the idea of the simple or complex feeling which it represents, that the association becomes indissoluble. No Englishman, for example, can think of the word "dog" without immediately having the idea of the group of impressions to which that name is given; and conversely, the group of impressions immediately calls up the idea of the word "dog."

The association of words with impressions and ideas is the process of naming; and language approaches perfection, in proportion as the shades of difference between various ideas and impressions are represented by differences in their names.

The names of simple impressions and ideas, or of groups of co-existent or successive complex impressions and ideas, considered per se, are substantives; as redness, dog, silver, mouth; while the names of impressions or ideas considered as parts or attributes of a complex whole, are adjectives. Thus redness, considered as part of the complex idea of a rose, becomes the adjective red; flesh-eater, as part of the idea of a dog, is represented by carnivorous; whiteness, as part of the idea of silver, is white; and so on.

The linguistic machinery for the expression of belief is called predication; and, as all beliefs express ideas of relation, we may say that the sign of predication is the verbal symbol of a feeling of relation. The words which serve to indicate predication are verbs. If I say "silver" and then "white," I merely utter two names; but if I interpose between them the verb "is," I express a belief in the co-existence of the feeling of whiteness with the other feelings which constitute the totality of the complex idea of silver; in other words, I predicate "whiteness" of silver.

In such a case as this, the verb expresses predication and nothing else, and is called a copula. But, in the great majority of verbs, the word is the sign of a complex idea, and the predication is expressed only by its form. Thus in "silver shines," the verb "to shine" is the sign for the feeling of brightness, and the mark of predication lies in the form "shine-s."

Another result is brought about by the forms of verbs. By slight modifications they are made to indicate that a belief, or predication, is a memory, or is an expectation. Thus "silver shone" expresses a memory; "silver will shine" an expectation.

The form of words which expresses a predication is a proposition. Hence, every predication is the verbal equivalent of a belief; and, as every belief is either an immediate consciousness, a memory, or an expectation, and as every expectation is traceable to a memory, it follows that, in the long run, all propositions express either immediate states of consciousness, or memories. The proposition which predicates A of X must mean either, that the fact is testified by my present consciousness, as when I say that two colours, visible at this moment, resemble one another; or that A is indissolubly associated with X in memory; or that A is indissolubly associated with X in expectation. But it has already been shown that expectation is only an expression of memory.

Hume does not discuss the nature of language, but so much of what remains to be said, concerning his philosophical tenets, turns upon the value and the origin of verbal propositions, that this summary sketch of the relations of language to the thinking process will probably not be deemed superfluous.

So large an extent of the field of thought is traversed by Hume, in his discussion of the verbal propositions in which mankind enshrine their beliefs, that it would be impossible to follow him throughout all the windings of his long journey, within the limits of this essay. I purpose, therefore, to limit myself to those propositions which concern--1. Necessary Truths; 2. The Order of Nature; 3. The Soul; 4. Theism; 5. The Passions and Volition; 6. The Principle of Morals.

Hume's views respecting necessary truths, and more particularly concerning causation, have, more than any other part of his teaching, contributed to give him a prominent place in the history of philosophy.

"All the objects of human reason and inquiry may naturally be divided into two kinds, to wit, relations of ideas and matters of fact. Of the first kind are the sciences of geometry, algebra, and arithmetic, and, in short, every affirmation which is either intuitively or demonstratively certain. That the square of the hypothenuse is equal to the square of the two sides, is a proposition which expresses a relation between these two figures. That three times five is equal to the half of thirty, expresses a relation between these numbers. Propositions of this kind are discoverable by the mere operation of thought without dependence on whatever is anywhere existent in the universe. Though there never were a circle or a triangle in nature, the truths demonstrated by Euclid would for ever retain their certainty and evidence.

"Matters of fact, which are the second objects of human reason, are not ascertained in the same manner, nor is an evidence of their truth, however great, of a like nature with the foregoing. The contrary of every matter of fact is still possible, because it can never imply a contradiction, and is conceived by the mind with the same facility and distinctness, as if ever so conformable to reality. That the sun will not rise to-morrow, is no less intelligible a proposition, and implies no more contradiction, than the affirmation, that it will rise. We should in vain, therefore, attempt to demonstrate its falsehood. Were it demonstratively false, it would imply a contradiction, and could never be distinctly conceived by the mind."--(IV. pp. 32, 33.)

The distinction here drawn between the truths of geometry and other kinds of truth is far less sharply indicated in the Treatise, but as Hume expressly disowns any opinions on these matters but such as are expressed in the Inquiry, we may confine ourselves to the latter; and it is needful to look narrowly into the propositions here laid down, as much stress has been laid upon Hume's admission that the truths of mathematics are intuitively and demonstratively certain; in other words, that they are necessary and, in that respect, differ from all other kinds of belief.

What is meant by the assertion that "propositions of this kind are discoverable by the mere operation of thought without dependence on what is anywhere existent in the universe"?

Suppose that there were no such things as impressions of sight and touch anywhere in the universe, what idea could we have even of a straight line, much less of a triangle and of the relations between its sides? The fundamental proposition of all Hume's philosophy is that ideas are copied from impressions; and, therefore, if there were no impressions of straight lines and triangles there could be no ideas of straight lines and triangles. But what we mean by the universe is the sum of our actual and possible impressions.

So, again, whether our conception of number is derived from relations of impressions in space or in time, the impressions must exist in nature, that is, in experience, before their relations can be perceived. Form and number are mere names for certain relations between matters of fact; unless a man had seen or felt the difference between a straight line and a crooked one, straight and crooked would have no more meaning to him, than red and blue to the blind.

The axiom, that things which are equal to the same are equal to one another, is only a particular case of the predication of similarity; if there were no impressions, it is obvious that there could be no predicates. But what is an existence in the universe but an impression?

If what are called necessary truths are rigidly analysed, they will be found to be of two kinds. Either they depend on the convention which underlies the possibility of intelligible speech, that terms shall always have the same meaning; or they are propositions the negation of which implies the dissolution of some association in memory or expectation, which is in fact indissoluble; or the denial of some fact of immediate consciousness.

The "necessary truth" A = A means that the perception which is called A shall always be called A. The "necessary truth" that "two straight lines cannot inclose a space," means that we have no memory, and can form no expectation of their so doing. The denial of the "necessary truth" that the thought now in my mind exists, involves the denial of consciousness.

To the assertion that the evidence of matter of fact, is not so strong as that of relations of ideas, it may be justly replied, that a great number of matters of fact are nothing but relations of ideas. If I say that red is unlike blue, I make an assertion concerning a relation of ideas; but it is also matter of fact, and the contrary proposition is inconceivable. If I remember[26] something that happened five minutes ago, that is matter of fact; and, at the same time, it expresses a relation between the event remembered and the present time. It is wholly inconceivable to me that the event did not happen, so that my assurance respecting it is as strong as that which I have respecting any other necessary truth. In fact, the man is either very wise or very virtuous, or very lucky, perhaps all three, who has gone through life without accumulating a store of such necessary beliefs which he would give a good deal to be able to disbelieve.

It would be beside the mark to discuss the matter further on the present occasion. It is sufficient to point out that, whatever may be the differences, between mathematical and other truths, they do not justify Hume's statement. And it is, at any rate, impossible to prove, that the cogency of mathematical first principles is due to anything more than these circumstances; that the experiences with which they are concerned are among the first which arise in the mind; that they are so incessantly repeated as to justify us, according to the ordinary laws of ideation, in expecting that the associations which they form will be of extreme tenacity; while the fact, that the expectations based upon them are always verified, finishes the process of welding them together.

Thus, if the axioms of mathematics are innate, nature would seem to have taken unnecessary trouble; since the ordinary process of association appears to be amply sufficient to confer upon them all the universality and necessity which they actually possess.

Whatever needless admissions Hume may have made respecting other necessary truths he is quite clear about the axiom of causation, "That whatever event has a beginning must have a cause;" whether and in what sense it is a necessary truth; and, that question being decided, whence it is derived.

With respect to the first question, Hume denies that it is a necessary truth, in the sense that we are unable to conceive the contrary. The evidence by which he supports this conclusion in the Inquiry, however, is not strictly relevant to the issue.

"No object ever discovers, by the qualities which appear to the senses, either the cause which produced it, or the effects which will arise from it; nor can our reason, unassisted by experience, ever draw any inference concerning real existence and matter of fact."--(IV. p. 35.)

Abundant illustrations are given of this assertion, which indeed cannot be seriously doubted; but it does not follow that, because we are totally unable to say what cause preceded, or what effect will succeed, any event, we do not necessarily suppose that the event had a cause and will be succeeded by an effect. The scientific investigator who notes a new phenomenon may be utterly ignorant of its cause, but he will, without hesitation, seek for that cause. If you ask him why he does so, he will probably say that it must have had a cause; and thereby imply that his belief in causation is a necessary belief.

In the Treatise Hume indeed takes the bull by the horns:

" ... as all distinct ideas are separable from each other, and as the ideas of cause and effect are evidently distinct, 'twill be easy for us to conceive any object to be non-existent this moment find existent the next, without conjoining to it the distinct idea of a cause or productive principle."--(I. p. 111.)

If Hume had been content to state what he believed to be matter of fact, and had abstained from giving superfluous reasons for that which is susceptible of being proved or disproved only by personal experience, his position would have been stronger. For it seems clear that, on the ground of observation, he is quite right. Any man who lets his fancy run riot in a waking dream, may experience the existence at one moment, and the non-existence at the next, of phenomena which suggest no connexion of cause and effect. Not only so, but it is notorious that, to the unthinking mass of mankind, nine-tenths of the facts of life do not suggest the relation of cause and effect; and they practically deny the existence of any such relation by attributing them to chance. Few gamblers but would stare if they were told that the falling of a die on a particular face is as much the effect of a definite cause as the fact of its falling; it is a proverb that "the wind bloweth where it listeth;" and even thoughtful men usually receive with surprise the suggestion, that the form of the crest of every wave that breaks, wind-driven, on the sea-shore, and the direction of every particle of foam that flies before the gale, are the exact effects of definite causes; and, as such, must be capable of being determined, deductively, from the laws of motion and the properties of air and water. So again, there are large numbers of highly intelligent persons who rather pride themselves on their fixed belief that our volitions have no cause; or that the will causes itself, which is either the same thing, or a contradiction in terms.

Hume's argument in support of what appears to be a true proposition, however, is of the circular sort, for the major premiss, that all distinct ideas are separable in thought, assumes the question at issue.

But the question whether the idea of causation is necessary, or not, is really of very little importance. For, to say that an idea is necessary is simply to affirm that we cannot conceive the contrary; and the fact that we cannot conceive the contrary of any belief may be a presumption, but is certainly no proof, of its truth.

In the well-known experiment of touching a single round object, such as a marble, with crossed fingers, it is utterly impossible to conceive that we have not two round objects under them; and, though light is undoubtedly a mere sensation arising in the brain, it is utterly impossible to conceive that it is not outside the retina. In the same way, he who touches anything with a rod, not only is irresistibly led to believe that the sensation of contact is at the end of the rod, but is utterly incapable of conceiving that this sensation is really in his head. Yet that which is inconceivable is manifestly true in all these cases. The beliefs and the unbeliefs are alike necessary, and alike erroneous.

It is commonly urged that the axiom of causation cannot be derived from experience, because experience only proves that many things have causes, whereas the axiom declares that all things have causes. The syllogism, "many things which come into existence have causes, A has come into existence: therefore A had a cause," is obviously fallacious, if A is not previously shown to be one of the "many things." And this objection is perfectly sound so far as it goes. The axiom of causation cannot possibly be deduced from any general proposition which simply embodies experience. But it does not follow that the belief, or expectation, expressed by the axiom, is not a product of experience, generated antecedently to, and altogether independently of, the logically unjustifiable language in which we express it.

In fact, the axiom of causation resembles all other beliefs of expectation in being the verbal symbol of a purely automatic act of the mind, which is altogether extra-logical, and would be illogical, if it were not constantly verified by experience. Experience, as we have seen, stores up memories; memories generate expectations or beliefs--why they do so may be explained hereafter by proper investigation of cerebral physiology. But, to seek for the reason of the facts in the verbal symbols by which they are expressed, and to be astonished that it is not to be found there, is surely singular; and what Hume did was to turn attention from the verbal proposition to the psychical fact of which it is the symbol.

"When any natural object or event is presented, it is impossible for us, by any sagacity or penetration, to discover, or even conjecture, without experience, what event will result from it, or to carry our foresight beyond that object, which is immediately present to the memory and senses. Even after one instance or experiment, where we have observed a particular event to follow upon another, we are not entitled to form a general rule, or foretell what will happen in like cases; it being justly esteemed an unpardonable temerity to judge of the whole course of nature from one single experiment, however accurate or certain. But when one particular species of events has always, in all instances, been conjoined with another, we make no longer any scruple of foretelling one upon the appearance of the other, and of employing that reasoning which can alone assure us of any matter of fact or existence. We then call the one object Cause, the other Effect. We suppose that there is some connexion between them: some power in the one, by which it infallibly produces the other, and operates with the greatest certainty and strongest necessity.... But there is nothing in a number of instances, different from every single instance, which is supposed to be exactly similar; except only, that after a repetition of similar instances, the mind is carried by habit, upon the appearance of one event, to expect its usual attendant, and to believe that it will exist.... The first time a man saw the communication of motion by impulse, as by the shock of two billiard balls, he could not pronounce that the one event was connected, but only that it was conjoined, with the other. After he has observed several instances of this nature, he then pronounces them to be connected. What alteration has happened to give rise to this new idea of connexion? Nothing but that he now feels those events to be connected in his imagination, and can readily foresee the existence of the one from the appearance of the other. When we say, therefore, that one object is connected with another we mean only that they have acquired a connexion in our thought, and give rise to this inference, by which they become proofs of each other's existence; a conclusion which is somewhat extraordinary, but which seems founded on sufficient evidence."-- (IV. pp. 87-89.)

In the fifteenth section of the third part of the Treatise, under the head of the Rules by which to Judge of Causes and Effects, Hume gives a sketch of the method of allocating effects to their causes, upon which, so far as I am aware, no improvement was made down to the time of the publication of Mill's Logic. Of Mill's four methods, that of agreement is indicated in the following passage:--

" ... where several different objects produce the same effect, it must be by means of some quality which we discover to be common amongst them. For as like effects imply like causes, we must always ascribe the causation to the circumstance wherein we discover the resemblance."--(I. p. 229.)

Next, the foundation of the method of difference is stated:--

"The difference in the effects of two resembling objects must proceed from that particular in which they differ. For, as like causes always produce like effects, when in any instance we find our expectation to be disappointed, we must conclude that this irregularity proceeds from some difference in the causes."--(I. p. 230.)

In the succeeding paragraph the method of concomitant variations is foreshadowed.

"When any object increases or diminishes with the increase or diminution of the cause, 'tis to be regarded as a compounded effect, derived from the union of the several different effects which arise from the several different parts of the cause. The absence or presence of one part of the cause is here supposed to be always attended with the absence or presence of a proportionable part of the effect. This constant conjunction sufficiently proves that the one part is the cause of the other. We must, however, beware not to draw such a conclusion from a few experiments."--(I. p. 230.)

Lastly, the following rule, though awkwardly stated, contains a suggestion of the method of residues:--

" ... an object which exists for any time in its full perfection without any effect, is not the sole cause of that effect, but requires to be assisted by some other principle, which may forward its influence and operation. For as like effects necessarily follow from like causes, and in a contiguous time and place, their separation for a moment shows that these causes are not complete ones."--(I. p. 230.)

In addition to the bare notion of necessary connexion between the cause and its effect, we undoubtedly find in our minds the idea of something resident in the cause which, as we say, produces the effect, and we call this something Force, Power, or Energy. Hume explains Force and Power as the results of the association with inanimate causes of the feelings of endeavour or resistance which we experience, when our bodies give rise to, or resist, motion.

If I throw a ball, I have a sense of effort which ends when the ball leaves my hand; and if I catch a ball, I have a sense of resistance which comes to an end with the quiescence of the ball. In the former case, there is a strong suggestion of something having gone from myself into the ball; in the latter, of something having been received from the ball. Let any one hold a piece of iron near a strong magnet, and the feeling that the magnet endeavours to pull the iron one way in the same manner as he endeavours to pull it in the opposite direction, is very strong.

As Hume says:--

"No animal can put external bodies in motion without the sentiment of a nisus, or endeavour; and every animal has a sentiment or feeling from the stroke or blow of an external object that is in motion. These sensations, which are merely animal, and from which we can, a priori, draw no inference, we are apt to transfer to inanimate objects, and to suppose that they have some such feelings whenever they transfer or receive motion."--(IV. p. 91, note.)

It is obviously, however, an absurdity not less gross than that of supposing the sensation of warmth to exist in a fire, to imagine that the subjective sensation of effort or resistance in ourselves can be present in external objects, when they stand in the relation of causes to other objects.

To the argument, that we have a right to suppose the relation of cause and effect to contain something more than invariable succession, because, when we ourselves act as causes, or in volition, we are conscious of exerting power; Hume replies, that we know nothing of the feeling we call power except as effort or resistance; and that we have not the slightest means of knowing whether it has anything to do with the production of bodily motion or mental changes. And he points out, as Descartes and Spinoza had done before him, that when voluntary motion takes place, that which we will is not the immediate consequence of the act of volition, but something which is separated from it by a long chain of causes and effects. If the will is the cause of the movement of a limb, it can be so only in the sense that the guard who gives the order to go on, is the cause of the transport of a train from one station to another.

"We learn from anatomy, that the immediate object of power in voluntary motion is not the member itself which is moved, but certain muscles and nerves and animal spirits, and perhaps something still more minute and unknown, through which the motion is successively propagated, ere it reach the member itself, whose motion is the immediate object of volition. Can there be a more certain proof that the power by which the whole operation is performed, so far from being directly and fully known by an inward sentiment or consciousness, is to the last degree mysterious and unintelligible? Here the mind wills a certain event: Immediately another event, unknown to ourselves, and totally different from the one intended, is produced: This event produces another equally unknown: Till at last, through a long succession, the desired event is produced."--(IV. p. 78.)

A still stronger argument against ascribing an objective existence to force or power, on the strength of our supposed direct intuition of power in voluntary acts, may be urged from the unquestionable fact, that we do not know, and cannot know, that volition does cause corporeal motion; while there is a great deal to be said in favour of the view that it is no cause, but merely a concomitant of that motion. But the nature of volition will be more fitly considered hereafter.

FOOTNOTE:

[26] Hume, however, expressly includes the "records of our memory" among his matters of fact.--(IV. p. 33.)

CHAPTER VII.

THE ORDER OF NATURE: MIRACLES.

If our beliefs of expectation are based on our beliefs of memory, and anticipation is only inverted recollection, it necessarily follows that every belief of expectation implies the belief that the future will have a certain resemblance to the past. From the first hour of experience, onwards, this belief is constantly being verified, until old age is inclined to suspect that experience has nothing new to offer. And when the experience of generation after generation is recorded, and a single book tells us more than Methuselah could have learned, had he spent every waking hour of his thousand years in learning; when apparent disorders are found to be only the recurrent pulses of a slow working order, and the wonder of a year becomes the commonplace of a century; when repeated and minute examination never reveals a break in the chain of causes and effects; and the whole edifice of practical life is built upon our faith in its continuity; the belief that that chain has never been broken and will never be broken, becomes one of the strongest and most justifiable of human convictions. And it must be admitted to be a reasonable request, if we ask those who would have us put faith in the actual occurrence of interruptions of that order, to produce evidence in favour of their view, not only equal, but superior, in weight to that which leads us to adopt ours.

This is the essential argument of Hume's famous disquisition upon miracles; and it may safely be declared to be irrefragable. But it must be admitted that Hume has surrounded the kernel of his essay with a shell of very doubtful value.

The first step in this, as in all other discussions, is to come to a clear understanding as to the meaning of the terms employed. Argumentation whether miracles are possible, and, if possible, credible, is mere beating the air until the arguers have agreed what they mean by the word "miracles."

Hume, with less than his usual perspicuity, but in accordance with a common practice of believers in the miraculous, defines a miracle as a "violation of the laws of nature," or as "a transgression of a law of nature by a particular volition of the Deity, or by the interposition of some invisible agent."

There must, he says,--

"be an uniform experience against every miraculous event, otherwise the event would not merit that appellation. And as an uniform experience amounts to a proof, there is here a direct and full proof, from the nature of the fact, against the existence of any miracle; nor can such a proof be destroyed or the miracle rendered credible but by an opposite proof which is superior."--(IV. p. 134.)

Every one of these dicta appears to be open to serious objection.

The word "miracle"--miraculum,--in its primitive and legitimate sense, simply means something wonderful.

Cicero applies it as readily to the fancies of philosophers, "Portenta et miracula philosophorum somniantium," as we do to the prodigies of priests. And the source of the wonder which a miracle excites is the belief, on the part of those who witness it, that it transcends or contradicts ordinary experience.

The definition of a miracle as a "violation of the laws of nature" is, in reality, an employment of language which, on the face of the matter, cannot be justified. For "nature" means neither more nor less than that which is; the sum of phenomena presented to our experience; the totality of events past, present, and to come. Every event must be taken to be a part of nature, until proof to the contrary is supplied. And such proof is, from the nature of the case, impossible.

Hume asks:--

"Why is it more than probable that all men must die: that lead cannot of itself remain suspended in the air: that fire consumes wood and is extinguished by water; unless it be that these events are found agreeable to the laws of nature, and there is required a violation of those laws, or in other words, a miracle, to prevent them?"--(IV. p. 133.)

But the reply is obvious; not one of these events is "more than probable"; though the probability may reach such a very high degree that, in ordinary language, we are justified in saying that the opposite events are impossible. Calling our often verified experience a "law of nature" adds nothing to its value, nor in the slightest degree increases any probability that it will be verified again, which may arise out of the fact of its frequent verification.

If a piece of lead were to remain suspended of itself, in the air, the occurrence would be a "miracle," in the sense of a wonderful event, indeed; but no one trained in the methods of science would imagine that any law of nature was really violated thereby. He would simply set to work to investigate the conditions under which so highly unexpected an occurrence took place, and thereby enlarge his experience and modify his hitherto unduly narrow conception of the laws of nature.

The alternative definition, that a miracle is "a transgression of a law of nature by a particular volition of the Deity, or by the interposition of some invisible agent," (IV. p. 134, note) is still less defensible. For a vast number of miracles have professedly been worked, neither by the Deity, nor by any invisible agent; but by Beelzebub and his compeers, or by very visible men.

Moreover, not to repeat what has been said respecting the absurdity of supposing that something which occurs is a transgression of laws, our only knowledge of which is derived from the observation of that which occurs; upon what sort of evidence can we be justified in concluding that a given event is the effect of a particular volition of the Deity, or of the interposition of some invisible (that is unperceivable) agent? It may be so, but how is the assertion, that it is so, to be tested? If it be said that the event exceeds the power of natural causes, what can justify such a saying? The day-fly has better grounds for calling a thunderstorm supernatural, than has man, with his experience of an infinitesimal fraction of duration, to say that the most astonishing event that can be imagined is beyond the scope of natural causes.

"Whatever is intelligible and can be distinctly conceived, implies no contradiction, and can never be proved false by any demonstration, argument, or abstract reasoning a priori."--(IV. p. 44.)

So wrote Hume, with perfect justice, in his Sceptical Doubts. But a miracle, in the sense of a sudden and complete change in the customary order of nature, is intelligible, can be distinctly conceived, implies no contradiction; and, therefore, according to Hume's own showing, cannot be proved false by any demonstrative argument.

Nevertheless, in diametrical contradiction to his own principles, Hume says elsewhere:--

"It is a miracle that a dead man should come to life: because that has never been observed in any age or country."--(IV. p. 134.)

That is to say, there is an uniform experience against such an event, and therefore, if it occurs, it is a violation of the laws of nature. Or, to put the argument in its naked absurdity, that which never has happened never can happen, without a violation of the laws of nature. In truth, if a dead man did come to life, the fact would be evidence, not that any law of nature had been violated, but that those laws, even when they express the results of a very long and uniform experience, are necessarily based on incomplete knowledge, and are to be held only as grounds of more or less justifiable expectation.

To sum up, the definition of a miracle as a suspension or a contravention of the order of Nature is self-contradictory, because all we know of the order of nature is derived from our observation of the course of events of which the so-called miracle is a part. On the other hand, no event is too extraordinary to be impossible; and, therefore, if by the term miracles we mean only "extremely wonderful events," there can be no just ground for denying the possibility of their occurrence.

But when we turn from the question of the possibility of miracles, however they may be defined, in the abstract, to that respecting the grounds upon which we are justified in believing any particular miracle, Hume's arguments have a very different value, for they resolve themselves into a simple statement of the dictates of common sense--which may be expressed in this canon: the more a statement of fact conflicts with previous experience, the more complete must be the evidence which is to justify us in believing it. It is upon this principle that every one carries on the business of common life. If a man tells me he saw a piebald horse in Piccadilly, I believe him without hesitation. The thing itself is likely enough, and there is no imaginable motive for his deceiving me. But if the same person tells me he observed a zebra there, I might hesitate a little about accepting his testimony, unless I were well satisfied, not only as to his previous acquaintance with zebras, but as to his powers and opportunities of observation in the present case. If, however, my informant assured me that he beheld a centaur trotting down that famous thoroughfare, I should emphatically decline to credit his statement; and this even if he were the most saintly of men and ready to suffer martyrdom in support of his belief. In such a case, I could, of course, entertain no doubt of the good faith of the witness; it would be only his competency, which unfortunately has very little to do with good faith or intensity of conviction, which I should presume to call in question.

Indeed, I hardly know what testimony would satisfy me of the existence of a live centaur. To put an extreme case, suppose the late Johannes M 黙 ler, of Berlin, the greatest anatomist and physiologist among my contemporaries, had barely affirmed he had seen a live centaur, I should certainly have been staggered by the weight of an assertion coming from such an authority. But I could have got no further than a suspension of judgment. For, on the whole, it would have been more probable that even he had fallen into some error of interpretation of the facts which came under his observation, than that such an animal as a centaur really existed. And nothing short of a careful monograph, by a highly competent investigator, accompanied by figures and measurements of all the most important parts of a centaur, put forth under circumstances which could leave no doubt that falsification or misinterpretation would meet with immediate exposure, could possibly enable a man of science to feel that he acted conscientiously, in expressing his belief in the existence of a centaur on the evidence of testimony.

This hesitation about admitting the existence of such an animal as a centaur, be it observed, does not deserve reproach, as scepticism, but moderate praise, as mere scientific good faith. It need not imply, and it does not, so far as I am concerned, any a priori hypothesis that a centaur is an impossible animal; or, that his existence, if he did exist, would violate the laws of nature. Indubitably, the organisation of a centaur presents a variety of practical difficulties to an anatomist and physiologist; and a good many of those generalisations of our present experience, which we are pleased to call laws of nature, would be upset by the appearance of such an animal, so that we should have to frame new laws to cover our extended experience. Every wise man will admit that the possibilities of nature are infinite, and include centaurs; but he will not the less feel it his duty to hold fast, for the present, by the dictum of Lucretius, "Nam certe ex vivo Centauri non fit imago," and to cast the entire burthen of proof, that centaurs exist, on the shoulders of those who ask him to believe the statement.

Judged by the canons either of common sense, or of science, which are indeed one and the same, all "miracles" are centaurs, or they would not be miracles; and men of sense and science will deal with them on the same principles. No one who wishes to keep well within the limits of that which he has a right to assert will affirm that it is impossible that the sun and moon should ever have been made to appear to stand still in the valley of Ajalon; or that the walls of a city should have fallen down at a trumpet blast; or that water was turned into wine; because such events are contrary to uniform experience and violate laws of nature. For aught he can prove to the contrary, such events may appear in the order of nature to-morrow. But common sense and common honesty alike oblige him to demand from those who would have him believe in the actual occurrence of such events, evidence of a cogency proportionate to their departure from probability; evidence at least as strong as that, which the man who says he has seen a centaur is bound to produce, unless he is content to be thought either more than credulous or less than honest.

But are there any miracles on record, the evidence for which fulfils the plain and simple requirements alike of elementary logic and of elementary morality?

Hume answers this question without the smallest hesitation, and with all the authority of a historical specialist:--

"There is not to be found, in all history, any miracle attested by a sufficient number of men, of such unquestioned goodness, education, and learning, as to secure us against all delusion in themselves; of such undoubted integrity, as to place them beyond all suspicion of any design to deceive others; of such credit and reputation in the eyes of mankind, as to have a great deal to lose in case of their being detected in any falsehood; and at the same time attesting facts, performed in such a public manner, and in so celebrated a part of the world, as to render the detection unavoidable: All which circumstances are requisite to give us a full assurance of the testimony of men."--(IV. p. 135.)

These are grave assertions, but they are least likely to be challenged by those who have made it their business to weigh evidence and to give their decision under a due sense of the moral responsibility which they incur in so doing.

It is probable that few persons who proclaim their belief in miracles have considered what would be necessary to justify that belief in the case of a professed modern miracle-worker. Suppose, for example, it is affirmed that

A.B. died and that C.D. brought him to life again. Let it be granted that A.B. and C.D. are persons of unimpeachable honour and veracity; that C.D. is the next heir to A.B.'s estate, and therefore had a strong motive for not bringing him to life again; and that all A.B.'s relations, respectable persons who bore him a strong affection, or had otherwise an interest in his being alive, declared that they saw him die. Furthermore, let A.B. be seen after his recovery by all his friends and neighbours, and let his and their depositions, that he is now alive, be taken down before a magistrate of known integrity and acuteness: would all this constitute even presumptive evidence that C.D. had worked a miracle? Unquestionably not. For the most important link in the whole chain of evidence is wanting, and that is the proof that A.B. was really dead. The evidence of ordinary observers on such a point as this is absolutely worthless. And, even medical evidence, unless the physician is a person of unusual knowledge and skill, may have little more value. Unless careful thermometric observation proves that the temperature has sunk below a certain point; unless the cadaveric stiffening of the muscles has become well established; all the ordinary signs of death may be fallacious, and the intervention of C.D. may have had no more to do with A.B.'s restoration to life than any other fortuitously coincident event.

It may be said that such a coincidence would be more wonderful than the miracle itself. Nevertheless history acquaints us with coincidences as marvellous.

On the 19th of February, 1842, Sir Robert Sale held Jellalabad with a small English force and, daily expecting attack from an overwhelming force of Afghans, had spent three months in incessantly labouring to improve the fortifications of the town. Akbar Khan had approached within a few miles, and an onslaught of his army was supposed to be imminent. That morning an earthquake--

"nearly destroyed the town, threw down the greater part of the parapets, the central gate with the adjoining bastions, and a part of the new bastion which flanked it. Three other bastions were also nearly destroyed, whilst several large breaches were made in the curtains, and the Peshawur side, eighty feet long, was quite practicable, the ditch being filled, and the descent easy. Thus in one moment the labours of three months were in a great measure destroyed."[27]

If Akbar Khan had happened to give orders for an assault in the early morning of the 19th of February, what good follower of the Prophet could have doubted that Allah had lent his aid? As it chanced, however, Mahometan faith in the miraculous took another turn; for the energetic defenders of the post had repaired the damage by the end of the month; and the enemy, finding no signs of the earthquake when they invested the place, ascribed the supposed immunity of Jellalabad to English witchcraft.

But the conditions of belief do not vary with time or place; and, if it is undeniable that evidence of so complete and weighty a character is needed, at the present time, for the establishment of the occurrence of such a wonder as that supposed, it has always been needful. Those who study the extant records of miracles with due attention will judge for themselves how far it has ever been supplied.

FOOTNOTE:

[27] Report of Captain Broadfoot, garrison engineer, quoted in Kaye's Afghanistan.

CHAPTER VIII.

THEISM; EVOLUTION OF THEOLOGY.

Hume seems to have had but two hearty dislikes: the one to the English nation, and the other to all the professors of dogmatic theology. The one aversion he vented only privately to his friends; but, if he is ever bitter in his public utterances, it is against priests[28] in general and theological enthusiasts and fanatics in particular; if he ever seems insincere, it is when he wishes to insult theologians by a parade of sarcastic respect. One need go no further than the peroration of the Essay on Miracles for a characteristic illustration.

"I am the better pleased with the method of reasoning here delivered, as I think it may serve to confound those dangerous friends and disguised enemies to the Christian religion who have undertaken to defend it by the principles of human reason. Our most holy religion is founded on Faith, not on reason, and it is a sure method of exposing it to put it to such a trial as it is by no means fitted to endure. ... the Christian religion not only was at first attended with miracles, but even at this day cannot be believed by any reasonable person without one. Mere reason is insufficient to convince us of its veracity: And whoever is moved by Faith to assent to it, is conscious of a continual miracle in his own person, which subverts all the principles of his understanding, and gives him a determination to believe what is most contrary to custom and experience."--(IV. pp. 153, 154.)

It is obvious that, here and elsewhere, Hume, adopting a popular confusion of ideas, uses religion as the equivalent of dogmatic theology; and, therefore, he says, with perfect justice, that "religion is nothing but a species of philosophy" (iv. p. 171). Here no doubt lies the root of his antagonism. The quarrels of theologians and philosophers have not been about religion, but about philosophy; and philosophers not unfrequently seem to entertain the same feeling towards theologians that sportsmen cherish towards poachers. "There cannot be two passions more nearly resembling each other than hunting and philosophy," says Hume. And philosophic hunters are given to think, that, while they pursue truth for its own sake, out of pure love for the chase (perhaps mingled with a little human weakness to be thought good shots), and by open and legitimate methods; their theological competitors too often care merely to supply the market of establishments; and disdain neither the aid of the snares of superstition, nor the cover of the darkness of ignorance.

Unless some foundation was given for this impression by the theological writers whose works had fallen in Hume's way, it is difficult to account for the depth of feeling which so good natured a man manifests on the subject.

Thus he writes in the Natural History of Religion, with quite unusual acerbity:-
-

"The chief objection to it [the ancient heathen mythology] with regard to this planet is, that it is not ascertained by any just reason or authority. The ancient tradition insisted on by heathen priests and theologers is but a weak foundation: and transmitted also such a number of contradictory reports, supported all of them by equal authority, that it became absolutely impossible to fix a preference among them. A few volumes, therefore, must contain all the polemical writings of pagan priests: And their whole theology must consist more of traditional stories and superstitious practices than of philosophical argument and controversy.

"But where theism forms the fundamental principle of any popular religion, that tenet is so conformable to sound reason, that philosophy is apt to incorporate itself with such a system of theology. And if the other dogmas of that system be contained in a sacred book, such as the Alcoran, or be determined by any visible authority, like that of the Roman pontiff, speculative reasoners naturally carry on their assent, and embrace a theory, which has been instilled into them by their earliest education, and which also possesses some degree of consistence and uniformity. But as these appearances are sure, all of them, to prove deceitful, philosophy will very soon find herself very unequally yoked with her new associate; and instead of regulating each principle, as they advance together, she is at every turn perverted to serve the purposes of superstition. For besides the unavoidable incoherences, which must be reconciled and adjusted, one may safely affirm, that all popular theology, especially the scholastic, has a kind of appetite for absurdity and contradiction. If that theology went not beyond reason and common sense, her doctrines would appear too easy and familiar. Amazement must of necessity be raised: Mystery affected: Darkness and obscurity sought after: And a foundation of merit afforded to the devout votaries, who desire an opportunity of subduing their rebellious reason by the belief of the most unintelligible sophisms.

"Ecclesiastical history sufficiently confirms these reflections. When a controversy is started, some people always pretend with certainty to foretell the issue. Whichever opinion, say they, is most contrary to plain reason is sure to prevail; even when the general interest of the system requires not that decision. Though the reproach of heresy may, for some time, be bandied about among the disputants, it always rests at last on the side of reason. Any one, it is pretended, that has but learning enough of this kind to know the definition of Arian, Pelagian, Erastian, Socinian, Sabellian, Eutychian, Nestorian, Monothelite, &c., not to mention Protestant, whose fate is yet uncertain, will be convinced of the truth of this observation. It is thus a system becomes absurd in the end, merely from its being reasonable and philosophical in the beginning.

"To oppose the torrent of scholastic religion by such feeble maxims as these, that it is impossible for the same thing to be and not to be, that the whole is greater than a part, that two and three make five, is pretending to stop the ocean with a bulrush. Will you set up profane reason against sacred mystery? No punishment is great enough for your impiety. And the same fires which were kindled for heretics will serve also for the destruction of philosophers."--(IV. pp. 481-3.)

Holding these opinions respecting the recognised systems of theology and their professors, Hume, nevertheless, seems to have had a theology of his own; that is to say, he seems to have thought (though, as will appear, it is needful for an expositor of his opinions to speak very guardedly on this point) that the problem of theism is susceptible of scientific treatment, with something more than a negative result. His opinions are to be gathered from the eleventh section of the Inquiry (1748); from the Dialogues concerning Natural Religion, which were written at least as early as 1751, though not published till after his death; and from the Natural History of Religion, published in 1757.

In the first two pieces, the reader is left to judge for himself which interlocutor in the dialogue represents the thoughts of the author; but, for the views put forward in the last, Hume accepts the responsibility. Unfortunately, this essay deals almost wholly with the historical development of theological ideas; and, on the question of the philosophical foundation of theology, does little more than express the writer's contentment with the argument from design.

"The whole frame of nature bespeaks an Intelligent Author; and no rational inquirer can, after serious reflection, suspend his belief a moment with regard to the primary principles of genuine Theism and Religion.--(IV. p. 435.)

"Were men led into the apprehension of invisible, intelligent power, by a contemplation of the works of nature, they could never possibly entertain any conception but of one single being, who bestowed existence and order on this vast machine, and adjusted all its parts according to one regular plan or connected system. For though, to persons of a certain turn of mind, it may not appear altogether absurd, that several independent beings, endowed with superior wisdom, might conspire in the contrivance and execution of one regular plan, yet is this a merely arbitrary supposition, which, even if allowed possible, must be confessed neither to be supported by probability nor necessity. All things in the universe are evidently of a piece. Everything is adjusted to everything. One design prevails throughout the whole. And this uniformity leads the mind to acknowledge one author; because the conception of different authors, without any distinction of attributes or operations, serves only to give perplexity to the imagination, without bestowing any satisfaction on the understanding."--(IV. p. 442.)

Thus Hume appears to have sincerely accepted the two fundamental conclusions of the argument from design; firstly, that a Deity exists; and, secondly, that He possesses attributes more or less allied to those of human intelligence. But, at this embryonic stage of theology, Hume's progress is arrested; and, after a survey of the development of dogma, his "general corollary" is, that--

"The whole is a riddle, an enigma, an inexplicable mystery. Doubt, uncertainty, suspense of judgment, appear the only result of our most accurate scrutiny concerning this subject. But such is the frailty of human reason, and such the irresistible contagion of opinion, that even this deliberate doubt could scarcely be upheld; did we not enlarge our view, and opposing one species of superstition to another, set them a quarrelling; while we ourselves, during their fury and contention, happily make our escape into the calm, though obscure, regions of philosophy."--(IV. p. 513.)

Thus it may be fairly presumed that Hume expresses his own sentiments in the words of the speech with which Philo concludes the Dialogues.

"If the whole of natural theology, as some people seem to maintain, resolves itself into one simple, though somewhat ambiguous, at least undefined proposition, That the cause or causes of order in the universe probably bear some remote analogy to human intelligence: If this proposition be not capable of extension, variation, or more particular explication: If it affords no inference that affects human life or can be the source of any action or forbearance: And if the analogy, imperfect as it is, can be carried no further than to the human intelligence, and cannot be transferred, with any appearance of probability, to the other qualities of the mind; if this really be the case, what can the most inquisitive, contemplative, and religious man do more than give a plain, philosophical assent to the proposition, as often as it occurs, and believe that the arguments on which it is established exceed the objections which lie against it? Some astonishment indeed will naturally arise from the greatness of the object; some melancholy from its obscurity; some contempt of human reason, that it can give no solution more satisfactory with regard to so extraordinary and magnificent a question. But believe me, Cleanthes, the most natural sentiment which a well-disposed mind will feel on this occasion, is a longing desire and expectation that Heaven would be pleased to dissipate, at least alleviate, this profound ignorance, by affording some more particular revelation to mankind, and making discoveries of the nature, attributes, and operations of the Divine object of our faith."[29]--(II. pp. 547-8.)

Such being the sum total of Hume's conclusions, it cannot be said that his theological burden is a heavy one. But, if we turn from the Natural History of Religion, to the Treatise, the Inquiry, and the Dialogues, the story of what happened to the ass laden with salt, who took to the water, irresistibly suggests itself. Hume's theism, such as it is, dissolves away in the dialectic river, until nothing is left but the verbal sack in which it was contained.

Of the two theistic propositions to which Hume is committed, the first is the affirmation of the existence of a God, supported by the argument from the nature of causation. In the Dialogues, Philo, while pushing scepticism to its utmost limit, is nevertheless made to say that--

" ... where reasonable men treat these subjects, the question can never be concerning the Being, but only the Nature, of the Deity. The former truth, as you will observe, is unquestionable and self-evident. Nothing exists without a cause, and the original cause of this universe (whatever it be) we call God, and piously ascribe to him every species of perfection."--(II. p. 439.)

The expositor of Hume, who wishes to do his work thoroughly, as far as it goes, cannot but fall into perplexity[30] when he contrasts this language with that of the sections of the third part of the Treatise, entitled, Why a Cause is Always Necessary, and Of the Idea of Necessary Connexion.

It is there shown, at large, that "every demonstration which has been produced for the necessity of a cause is fallacious and sophistical" (I. p. 111);

it is affirmed, that "there is no absolute nor metaphysical necessity that every beginning of existence should be attended with such an object" [as a cause] (I. p. 227); and it is roundly asserted, that it is "easy for us to conceive any object to be non-existent this moment and existent the next, without conjoining to it the distinct idea of a cause or productive principle" (I. p. 111). So far from the axiom, that whatever begins to exist must have a cause of existence, being "self-evident," as Philo calls it, Hume spends the greatest care in showing that it is nothing but the product of custom, or experience.

And the doubt thus forced upon one, whether Philo ought to be taken as even, so far, Hume's mouth-piece, is increased when we reflect that we are dealing with an acute reasoner; and that there is no difficulty in drawing the deduction from Hume's own definition of a cause, that the very phrase, a "first cause," involves a contradiction in terms. He lays down that,--

"'Tis an established axiom both in natural and moral philosophy, that an object, which exists for any time in its full perfection without producing another, is not its sole cause; but is assisted by some other principle which pushes it from its state of inactivity, and makes it exert that energy, of which it was secretly possessed."--(I. p. 106.)

Now the "first cause" is assumed to have existed from all eternity, up to the moment at which the universe came into existence. Hence it cannot be the sole cause of the universe; in fact, it was no cause at all until it was "assisted by some other principle"; consequently the so-called "first cause," so far as it produces the universe, is in reality an effect of that other principle. Moreover, though, in the person of Philo, Hume assumes the axiom "that whatever begins to exist must have a cause," which he denies in the Treatise, he must have seen, for a child may see, that the assumption is of no real service.

Suppose Y to be the imagined first cause and Z to be its effect. Let the letters of the alphabet, a, b, c, d, e, f, g, in their order, represent successive moments of time, and let g represent the particular moment at which the effect Z makes its appearance. It follows that the cause Y could not have existed "in its full perfection" during the time a--e, for if it had, then the effect Z would have come into existence during that time, which, by the hypothesis, it did not do. The cause Y, therefore, must have come into existence at f, and if "everything that comes into existence has a cause," Y must have had a cause

X operating at e; X, a cause W operating at d; and, so on, ad infinitum.[31]

If the only demonstrative argument for the existence of a Deity, which Hume advances, thus, literally, "goes to water" in the solvent of his philosophy, the reasoning from the evidence of design does not fare much better. If Hume really knew of any valid reply to Philo's arguments in the following passages of the Dialogues, he has dealt unfairly by the leader in concealing it:--

"But because I know you are not much swayed by names and authorities, I shall endeavour to show you, a little more distinctly, the inconveniences of that Anthropomorphism, which you have embraced; and shall prove, that there is no ground to suppose a plan of the world to be formed in the Divine mind, consisting of distinct ideas, differently arranged, in the same manner as an architect forms in his head the plan of a house which he intends to execute.

"It is not easy, I own, to see what is gained by this supposition, whether we judge the matter by Reason or by Experience. We are still obliged to mount higher, in order to find the cause of this cause, which you had assigned as satisfactory and conclusive.

"If Reason (I mean abstract reason, derived from inquiries a priori) be not alike mute with regard to all questions concerning cause and effect, this sentence at least it will venture to pronounce: That a mental world, or universe of ideas, requires a cause as much as does a material world, or universe of objects; and, if similar in its arrangement, must require a similar cause. For what is there in this subject, which should occasion a different conclusion or inference? In an abstract view, they are entirely alike; and no difficulty attends the one supposition, which is not common to both of them.

"Again, when we will needs force Experience to pronounce some sentence, even on those subjects which lie beyond her sphere, neither can she perceive any material difference in this particular, between these two kinds of worlds; but finds them to be governed by similar principles, and to depend upon an equal variety of causes in their operations. We have specimens in miniature of both of them. Our own mind resembles the one; a vegetable or animal body the other. Let experience, therefore, judge from these samples. Nothing seems more delicate, with regard to its causes, than thought: and as these causes never operate in two persons after the same manner, so we never find two persons who think exactly alike. Nor indeed does the same person think exactly alike at any two different periods of time. A difference of age, of the disposition of his body, of weather, of food, of company, of books, of passions; any of these particulars, or others more minute, are sufficient to alter the curious machinery of thought, and communicate to it very different movements and operations. As far as we can judge, vegetables and animal bodies are not more delicate in their motions, nor depend upon a greater variety or more curious adjustment of springs and principles.

"How, therefore, shall we satisfy ourselves concerning the cause of that Being whom you suppose the Author of Nature, or, according to your system of anthropomorphism, the ideal world in which you trace the material? Have we not the same reason to trace the ideal world into another ideal world, or new intelligent principle? But if we stop and go no farther; why go so far? Why not stop at the material world? How can we satisfy ourselves without going on in infinitum? And after all, what satisfaction is there in that infinite progression? Let us remember the story of the Indian philosopher and his elephant. It was never more applicable than to the present subject. If the material world rests upon a similar ideal world, this ideal world must rest upon some other; and so on without end. It were better, therefore, never to look beyond the present material world. By supposing it to contain the principle of its order within itself, we really assert it to be God; and the sooner we arrive at that Divine Being, so much the better. When you go one step beyond the mundane system you only excite an inquisitive humour, which it is impossible ever to satisfy.

"To say, that the different ideas which compose the reason of the Supreme Being, fall into order of themselves and by their own natures, is really to talk without any precise meaning. If it has a meaning, I would fain know why it is not as good sense to say, that the parts of the material world fall into order of themselves, and by their own nature. Can the one opinion be intelligible while the other is not so?"--(II. pp. 461-4.)

Cleanthes, in replying to Philo's discourse, says that it is very easy to answer his arguments; but, as not unfrequently happens with controversialists, he mistakes a reply for an answer, when he declares that--

"The order and arrangement of nature, the curious adjustment of final causes, the plain use and intention of every part and organ; all these bespeak in the clearest language one intelligent cause or author. The heavens and the earth join in the same testimony. The whole chorus of nature raises one hymn to the praises of its Creator."--(II. p. 465.)

Though the rhetoric of Cleanthes may be admired, its irrelevancy to the point at issue must be admitted. Wandering still further into the region of declamation, he works himself into a passion:

"You alone, or almost alone, disturb this general harmony. You start abstruse doubts, cavils, and objections: You ask me what is the cause of this cause? I know not: I care not: that concerns not me. I have found a Deity; and here I stop my inquiry. Let those go further who are wiser or more enterprising."--(II. p. 466.)

In other words, O Cleanthes, reasoning having taken you as far as you want to go, you decline to advance any further; even though you fully admit that the very same reasoning forbids you to stop where you are pleased to cry halt! But this is simply forcing your reason to abdicate in favour of your caprice. It is impossible to imagine that Hume, of all men in the world, could have rested satisfied with such an act of high-treason against the sovereignty of philosophy. We may rather conclude that the last word of the discussion, which he gives to Philo, is also his own.

"If I am still to remain in utter ignorance of causes, and can absolutely give an explication of nothing, I shall never esteem it any advantage to shove off for a moment a difficulty, which, you acknowledge, must immediately, in its full force, recur upon me. Naturalists[32] indeed very justly explain particular effects by more general causes, though these general causes should remain in the end totally inexplicable; but they never surely thought it satisfactory to explain a particular effect by a particular cause, which was no more to be accounted for than the effect itself. An ideal system, arranged of itself, without a precedent design, is not a whit more explicable than a material one, which attains its order in a like manner; nor is there any more difficulty in the latter supposition than in the former."--(II. p. 466.)

It is obvious that, if Hume had been pushed, he must have admitted that his opinion concerning the existence of a God, and of a certain remote resemblance of his intellectual nature to that of man, was an hypothesis which might possess more or less probability, but was incapable on his own principles of any approach to demonstration. And to all attempts to make any practical use of his theism; or to prove the existence of the attributes of infinite wisdom, benevolence, justice, and the like, which are usually ascribed to the Deity, by reason, he opposes a searching critical negation.[33]

The object of the speech of the imaginary Epicurean in the eleventh section of the Inquiry, entitled Of a Particular Providence and of a Future State, is to invert the argument of Bishop Butler's Analogy.

That famous defence of theology against the a priori scepticism of Freethinkers of the eighteenth century, who based their arguments on the inconsistency of the revealed scheme of salvation with the attributes of the Deity, consists, essentially, in conclusively proving that, from a moral point of view, Nature is at least as reprehensible as orthodoxy. If you tell me, says Butler, in effect, that any part of revealed religion must be false because it is inconsistent with the divine attributes of justice and mercy; I beg leave to point out to you, that there are undeniable natural facts which are fully open to the same objection. Since you admit that nature is the work of God, you are forced to allow that such facts are consistent with his attributes. Therefore, you must also admit, that the parallel facts in the scheme of orthodoxy are also consistent with them, and all your arguments to the contrary fall to the ground. Q.E.D. In fact, the solid sense of Butler left the Deism of the Freethinkers not a leg to stand upon. Perhaps, however, he did not remember the wise saying that "A man seemeth right in his own cause, but another cometh after and judgeth him." Hume's Epicurean philosopher adopts the main arguments of the Analogy, but unfortunately drives them home to a conclusion of which the good Bishop would hardly have approved.

"I deny a Providence, you say, and supreme governor of the world, who guides the course of events, and punishes the vicious with infamy and disappointment, and rewards the virtuous with honour and success in all their undertakings. But surely I deny not the course itself of events, which lies open to every one's inquiry and examination. I acknowledge that, in the present order of things, virtue is attended with more peace of mind than vice, and meets with a more favourable reception from the world. I am sensible that, according to the past experience of mankind, friendship is the chief joy of human life, and moderation the only source of tranquillity and happiness. I never balance between the virtuous and the vicious course of life; but am sensible that, to a well-disposed mind, every advantage is on the side of the former. And what can you say more, allowing all your suppositions and reasonings? You tell me, indeed, that this disposition of things proceeds from intelligence and design. But, whatever it proceeds from, the disposition itself, on which depends our happiness and misery, and consequently our conduct and deportment in life, is still the same. It is still open for me, as well as you, to regulate my behaviour by my experience of past events. And if you affirm that, while a divine providence is allowed, and a supreme distributive justice in the universe, I ought to expect some more particular reward of the good, and punishment of the bad, beyond the ordinary course of events, I here find the same fallacy which I have before endeavoured to detect. You persist in imagining, that if we grant that divine existence for which you so earnestly contend, you may safely infer consequences from it, and add something to the experienced order of nature, by arguing from the attributes which you ascribe to your gods. You seem not to remember that all your reasonings on this subject can only be drawn from effects to causes; and that every argument, deduced from causes to effects, must of necessity be a gross sophism, since it is impossible for you to know anything of the cause, but what you have antecedently not inferred, but discovered to the full, in the effect.

"But what must a philosopher think of those vain reasoners who, instead of regarding the present scene of things as the sole object of their contemplation, so far reverse the whole course of nature, as to render this life merely a passage to something further; a porch, which leads to a greater and vastly different building; a prologue which serves only to introduce the piece, and give it more grace and propriety? Whence, do you think, can such philosophers derive their idea of the gods? From their own conceit and imagination surely. For if they derive it from the present phenomena, it would never point to anything further, but must be exactly adjusted to them. That the divinity may possibly be endowed with attributes which we have never seen exerted; may be governed by principles of action which we cannot discover to be satisfied; all this will freely be allowed. But still this is mere possibility and hypothesis. We never can have reason to infer any attributes or any principles of action in him, but so far as we know them to have been exerted and satisfied.

"Are there any marks of a distributive justice in the world? If you answer in the affirmative, I conclude that, since justice here exerts itself, it is satisfied. If you reply in the negative, I conclude that you have then no reason to ascribe justice, in our sense of it, to the gods. If you hold a medium between affirmation and negation, by saying that the justice of the gods at present exerts itself in part, but not in its full extent, I answer that you have no reason to give it any particular extent, but only so far as you see it, at present, exert itself."--(IV. pp. 164-6.)

Thus, the Freethinkers said, the attributes of the Deity being what they are, the scheme of orthodoxy is inconsistent with them; whereupon Butler gave the crushing reply: Agreeing with you as to the attributes of the Deity, nature, by its existence, proves that the things to which you object are quite consistent with them. To whom enters Hume's Epicurean with the remark: Then, as nature is our only measure of the attributes of the Deity in their practical manifestation, what warranty is there for supposing that such measure is anywhere transcended? That the "other side" of nature, if there be one, is governed on different principles from this side?

Truly on this topic silence is golden; while speech reaches not even the dignity of sounding brass or tinkling cymbal, and is but the weary clatter of an endless logomachy. One can but suspect that Hume also had reached this conviction; and that his shadowy and inconsistent theism was the expression of his desire to rest in a state of mind, which distinctly excluded negation, while it included as little as possible of affirmation, respecting a problem which he felt to be hopelessly insoluble.

But, whatever might be the views of the philosopher as to the arguments for theism, the historian could have no doubt respecting its many-shaped existence, and the great part which it has played in the world. Here, then, was a body of natural facts to be investigated scientifically, and the result of Hume's inquiries is embodied in the remarkable essay on the Natural History of Religion. Hume anticipated the results of modern investigation in declaring fetishism and polytheism to be the form in which savage and ignorant men naturally clothe their ideas of the unknown influences which govern their destiny; and they are polytheists rather than monotheists because,--

" ... the first ideas of religion arose, not from a contemplation of the works of nature, but from a concern with regard to the events of life, and from the incessant hopes and fears which actuate the human mind ... in order to carry men's attention beyond the present course of things, or lead them into any inference concerning invisible intelligent power, they must be actuated by some passion which prompts their thought and reflection, some motive which urges their first inquiry. But what passion shall we have recourse to, for explaining an effect of such mighty consequence? Not speculative curiosity merely, or the pure love of truth. That motive is too refined for such gross apprehensions, and would lead men into inquiries concerning the frame of nature, a subject too large and comprehensive for their narrow capacities. No passions, therefore, can be supposed to work on such barbarians, but the ordinary affections of human life; the anxious concern for happiness, the dread of future misery, the terror of death, the thirst of revenge, the appetite for food and other necessaries. Agitated by hopes and fears of this nature, especially the latter, men scrutinize, with a trembling curiosity, the course of future causes, and examine the various and contrary events of human life. And in this disordered scene, with eyes still more disordered and astonished, they see the first obscure traces of divinity."--(IV. pp. 443, 4.)

The shape assumed by these first traces of divinity is that of the shadows of men's own minds, projected out of themselves by their imaginations:--

"There is an universal tendency among mankind to conceive all beings like themselves, and to transfer to every object those qualities with which they are familiarly acquainted, and of which they are intimately conscious.... The unknown causes which continually employ their thought, appearing always in the same aspect, are all apprehended to be of the same kind or species. Nor is it long before we ascribe to them thought, and reason, and passion, and sometimes even the limbs and figures of men, in order to bring them nearer to a resemblance with ourselves."--(IV. pp. 446-7.)

Hume asks whether polytheism really deserves the name of theism.

"Our ancestors in Europe, before the revival of letters, believed as we do at present, that there was one supreme God, the author of nature, whose power, though in itself uncontrollable, was yet often exerted by the interposition of his angels and subordinate ministers, who executed his sacred purposes. But they also believed, that all nature was full of other invisible powers: fairies, goblins, elves, sprights; beings stronger and mightier than men, but much inferior to the celestial natures who surround the throne of God. Now, suppose that any one, in these ages, had denied the existence of God and of his angels, would not his impiety justly have deserved the appellation of atheism, even though he had still allowed, by some odd capricious reasoning, that the popular stories of elves and fairies were just and well grounded? The difference, on the one hand, between such a person and a genuine theist, is infinitely greater than that, on the other, between him and one that absolutely excludes all invisible intelligent power. And it is a fallacy, merely from the casual resemblance of names, without any conformity of meaning, to rank such opposite opinions under the same denomination.

"To any one who considers justly of the matter, it will appear that the gods of the polytheists are no better than the elves and fairies of our ancestors, and merit as little as any pious worship and veneration. These pretended religionists are really a kind of superstitious atheists, and acknowledge no being that corresponds to our idea of a Deity. No first principle of mind or thought; no supreme government and administration; no divine contrivance or intention in the fabric of the world."--(IV. pp. 450-51.)

The doctrine that you may call an atheist anybody whose ideas about the Deity do not correspond with your own, is so largely acted upon by persons who are certainly not of Hume's way of thinking and, probably, so far from having read him, would shudder to open any book bearing his name, except the History of England, that it is surprising to trace the theory of their practice to such a source.

But on thinking the matter over, this theory seems so consonant with reason, that one feels ashamed of having suspected many excellent persons of being moved by mere malice and viciousness of temper to call other folks atheists, when, after all, they have been obeying a purely intellectual sense of fitness. As Hume says, truly enough, it is a mere fallacy, because two people use the same names for things, the ideas of which are mutually exclusive, to rank such opposite opinions under the same denomination. If the Jew says, that the Deity is absolute unity, and that it is sheer blasphemy to say that He ever became incarnate in the person of a man; and, if the Trinitarian says, that the Deity is numerically three as well as numerically one, and that it is sheer blasphemy to say that He did not so become incarnate, it is obvious enough that each must be logically held to deny the existence of the other's Deity. Therefore; that each has a scientific right to call the other an atheist; and that, if he refrains, it is only on the ground of decency and good manners, which should restrain an honourable man from employing even scientifically justifiable language, if custom has given it an abusive connotation. While one must agree with Hume, then, it is, nevertheless, to be wished that he had not set the bad example of calling polytheists "superstitious atheists." It probably did not occur to him that, by a parity of reasoning, the Unitarians might justify the application of the same language to the Ultramontanes, and vice vers? But, to return from a digression which may not be wholly unprofitable, Hume proceeds to show in what manner polytheism incorporated physical and moral allegories, and naturally accepted hero-worship; and he sums up his views of the first stages of the evolution of theology as follows:--

"These then are the general principles of polytheism, founded in human nature, and little or nothing dependent on caprice or accident. As the causes which bestow happiness or misery, are in general very little known and very uncertain, our anxious concern endeavours to attain a determinate idea of them: and finds no better expedient than to represent them as intelligent, voluntary agents, like ourselves, only somewhat superior in power and wisdom. The limited influence of these agents, and their proximity to human weakness, introduce the various distribution and division of their authority, and thereby give rise to allegory. The same principles naturally deify mortals, superior in power, courage, or understanding, and produce hero-worship; together with fabulous history and mythological tradition, in all its wild and unaccountable forms. And as an invisible spiritual intelligence is an object too refined for vulgar apprehension, men naturally affix it to some sensible representation; such as either the more conspicuous parts of nature, or the statues, images, and pictures, which a more refined age forms of its divinities."--(IV. p. 461.)

How did the further stage of theology, monotheism, arise out of polytheism? Hume replies, certainly not by reasonings from first causes or any sort of fine-drawn logic:--

"Even at this day, and in Europe, ask any of the vulgar why he believes in an Omnipotent Creator of the world, he will never mention the beauty of final causes, of which he is wholly ignorant: He will not hold out his hand and bid you contemplate the suppleness and variety of joints in his fingers, their bending all one way, the counterpoise which they receive from the thumb, the softness and fleshy parts of the inside of the hand, with all the other circumstances which render that member fit for the use to which it was destined. To these he has been long accustomed; and he beholds them with listlessness and unconcern. He will tell you of the sudden and unexpected death of such-a-one; the fall and bruise of such another; the excessive drought of this season; the cold and rains of another. These he ascribes to the immediate operation of Providence: And such events as, with good reasoners, are the chief difficulties in admitting a Supreme Intelligence, are with him the sole arguments for it....

"We may conclude therefore, upon the whole, that since the vulgar, in nations which have embraced the doctrine of theism, still build it upon irrational and superstitious grounds, they are never led into that opinion by any process of argument, but by a certain train of thinking, more suitable to their genius and capacity.

"It may readily happen, in an idolatrous nation, that though men admit the existence of several limited deities, yet there is some one God, whom, in a particular manner, they make the object of their worship and adoration. They may either suppose, that, in the distribution of power and territory among the Gods, their nation was subjected to the jurisdiction of that particular deity; or, reducing heavenly objects to the model of things below, they may represent one god as the prince or supreme magistrate of the rest, who, though of the same nature, rules them with an authority like that which an earthly sovereign exerts over his subjects and vassals. Whether this god, therefore, be considered as their peculiar patron, or as the general sovereign of heaven, his votaries will endeavour, by every art, to insinuate themselves into his favour; and supposing him to be pleased, like themselves, with praise and flattery, there is no eulogy or exaggeration which will be spared in their addresses to him. In proportion as men's fears or distresses become more urgent, they still invent new strains of adulation; and even he who outdoes his predecessor in swelling the titles of his divinity, is sure to be outdone by his successor in newer and more pompous epithets of praise. Thus they proceed, till at last they arrive at infinity itself, beyond which there is no further progress; And it is well if, in striving to get further, and to represent a magnificent simplicity, they run not into inexplicable mystery, and destroy the intelligent nature of their deity, on which alone any rational worship or adoration can be founded. While they confine themselves to the notion of a perfect being, the Creator of the world, they coincide, by chance, with the principles of reason and true philosophy; though they are guided to that notion, not by reason, of which they are in a great measure incapable, but by the adulation and fears of the most vulgar superstition."--(IV. pp. 463-6.)

"Nay, if we should suppose, what never happens, that a popular religion were found, in which it was expressly declared, that nothing but morality could gain the divine favour; if an order of priests were instituted to inculcate this opinion, in daily sermons, and with all the arts of persuasion; yet so inveterate are the people's prejudices, that, for want of some other superstition, they would make the very attendance on these sermons the essentials of religion, rather than place them in virtue and good morals. The sublime prologue of Zaleucus' laws inspired not the Locrians, so far as we can learn, with any sounder notions of the measures of acceptance with the deity, than were familiar to the other Greeks."--(IV. p. 505.)

It has been remarked that Hume's writings are singularly devoid of local colour; of allusions to the scenes with which, he was familiar, and to the people from whom he sprang. Yet, surely, the Lowlands of Scotland were more in his thoughts than the Zephyrean promontory, and the hard visage of John Knox peered from behind the mask of Zaleucus, when this passage left his pen. Nay, might not an acute German critic discern therein a reminiscence of that eminently Scottish institution, a "Holy Fair"? where as Hume's young contemporary sings:--

"... opens out his cauld harangues On practice and on morals; An' aff the godly pour in thrangs To gie the jars and barrels A lift that day.

"What signifies his barren shine Of moral powers and reason? His English style and gesture line Are a' clean out of season. Like Socrates or Antonine, Or some auld pagan heathen, The moral man he does define, But ne'er a word o' faith in That's right that day."[34]

FOOTNOTES:

[28] In a note to the Essay on Superstition and Enthusiasm, Hume is careful to define what he means by this term. "By priests I understand only the pretenders to power and dominion, and to a superior sanctity of character, distinct from virtue and good morals. These are very different from clergymen, who are set apart to the care of sacred matters, and the conducting our public devotions with greater decency and order. There is no rank of men more to be respected than the latter."--(III. p. 83.)

[29] It is needless to quote the rest of the passage, though I cannot refrain from observing that the recommendation which it contains, that a "man of letters" should become a philosophical sceptic as "the first and most essential step towards being a sound believing Christian," though adopted and largely acted upon by many a champion of orthodoxy in these days, is questionable in taste, if it be meant as a jest, and more than questionable in morality, if it is to be taken in earnest. To pretend that you believe any doctrine for no better reason than that you doubt everything else, would be dishonest, if it were not preposterous.

[30] A perplexity which is increased rather than diminished by some passages in a letter to Gilbert Elliot of Minto (March 10, 1751). Hume says, "You would perceive by the sample I have given you that I make Cleanthes the hero of the dialogue; whatever you can think of, to strengthen that side of the argument, will be most acceptable to me. Any propensity you imagine I have to the other side crept in upon me against my will; and 'tis not long ago that I burned an old manuscript book, wrote before I was twenty, which contained, page after page, the gradual progress of my thoughts on this head. It began with an anxious scent after arguments to confirm the common opinion; doubts stole in, dissipated, returned; were again dissipated, returned again; and it was a perpetual struggle of a restless imagination against inclination--perhaps against reason.... I could wish Cleanthes' argument could be so analysed as to be rendered quite formal and regular. The propensity of the mind towards it--unless that propensity were as strong and universal as that to believe in our senses and experience--will still, I am afraid, be esteemed a suspicious foundation. 'Tis here I wish for your assistance. We must endeavour to prove that this propensity is somewhat different from our

inclination to find our own figures in the clouds, our faces in the moon, our passions and sentiments even in inanimate matter. Such an inclination may and ought to be controlled, and can never be a legitimate ground of assent." (Burton, Life, I. pp. 331-3.) The picture of Hume here drawn unconsciously by his own hand, is unlike enough to the popular conception of him as a careless sceptic loving doubt for doubt's sake.

[31] Kant employs substantially the same argument:.

[32] I.e. Natural philosophers.

[33] Hume's letter to Mure of Caldwell, containing a criticism of Leechman's sermon (Burton, I. p. 163), bears strongly on this point.

[34] Burns published the Holy Fair only ten years after Hume's death.

CHAPTER IX.

THE SOUL: THE DOCTRINE OF IMMORTALITY.

Descartes taught that an absolute difference of kind separates matter, as that which possesses extension, from spirit, as that which thinks. They not only have no character in common, but it is inconceivable that they should have any. On the assumption, that the attributes of the two were wholly different, it appeared to be a necessary consequence that the hypothetical causes of these attributes--their respective substances--must be totally different. Notably, in the matter of divisibility, since that which has no extension cannot be divisible, it seemed that the chose pensante, the soul, must be an indivisible entity.

Later philosophers, accepting this notion of the soul, were naturally much perplexed to understand how, if matter and spirit had nothing in common, they could act and react on one another. All the changes of matter being modes of motion, the difficulty of understanding how a moving extended material body was to affect a thinking thing which had no dimension, was as great as that involved in solving the problem of how to hit a nominative case with a stick. Hence, the successors of Descartes either found themselves obliged, with the Occasionalists, to call in the aid of the Deity, who was supposed to be a sort of go-between betwixt matter and spirit; or they had recourse, with Leibnitz, to the doctrine of pre-established harmony, which denied any influence of the body on the soul, or vice vers? and compared matter and spirit to two clocks so accurately regulated to keep time with one another, that the one struck when ever the other pointed to the hour; or, with Berkeley, they abolished the "substance" of matter altogether, as a superfluity, though they failed to see that the same arguments equally justified the abolition of soul as another superfluity, and the reduction of the universe to a series of events or phenomena; or, finally, with Spinoza, to whom Berkeley makes a perilously close approach, they asserted the existence of only one substance, with two chief attributes, the one, thought, and the other, extension.

There remained only one possible position, which, had it been taken up earlier, might have saved an immensity of trouble; and that was to affirm that we do not, and cannot, know anything about the "substance" either of the thinking thing, or of the extended thing. And Hume's sound common sense led him to defend this thesis, which Locke had already foreshadowed, with respect to the question of the substance of the soul. Hume enunciates two opinions. The first is that the question itself is unintelligible, and therefore cannot receive any answer; the second is that the popular doctrine respecting the immateriality, simplicity, and indivisibility of a thinking substance is a "true atheism, and will serve to justify all those sentiments for which Spinoza is so universally infamous."

In support of the first opinion, Hume points out that it is impossible to attach any definite meaning to the word "substance" when employed for the hypothetical substratum of soul and matter. For if we define substance as that which may exist by itself, the definition does not distinguish the soul from perceptions. It is perfectly easy to conceive that states of consciousness are self-subsistent. And, if the substance of the soul is defined as that in which perceptions inhere, what is meant by the inherence? Is such inherence conceivable? It conceivable, what evidence is there of it? And what is the use of a substratum to things which, for anything we know to the contrary, are capable of existing by themselves?

Moreover, it may be added, supposing the soul has a substance, how do we know that it is different from the substance, which, on like grounds, must be supposed to underlie the qualities of matter?

Again, if it be said that our personal identity requires the assumption of a substance which remains the same while the accidents of perception shift and change, the question arises what is meant by personal identity?

"For my part," says Hume, "when I enter most intimately into what I call myself, I always stumble on some particular perception or other, of heat or cold, light or shade, love or hatred, pain or pleasure. I never can catch myself at any time without a perception, and never can observe anything but the perception. When my perceptions are removed for any time, as by sound sleep, so long am I insensible of myself, and may be truly said not to exist. And were all my perceptions removed by death, and I could neither think, nor feel, nor see, nor love, nor hate, after the dissolution of my body, I should be entirely annihilated, nor do I conceive what is further requisite to make me a perfect nonentity. If any one, upon serious and unprejudiced reflection, thinks he has a different notion of himself, I must confess I can reason no longer with him. All I can allow him is, that he may be in the right as well as I, and that we are essentially different in this particular. He may perhaps perceive something simple and continued which he calls himself, though I am certain there is no such principle in me.

"But setting aside some metaphysicians of this kind, I may venture to affirm of the rest of mankind, that they are nothing but a bundle or collection of different perceptions, which succeed one another with an inconceivable rapidity, and are in a perpetual flux and movement.... The mind is a kind of theatre, where several perceptions successively make their appearance, pass, repass, glide away, and mingle in an infinite variety of postures and situations. There is properly no simplicity in it at one time, nor identity in different, whatever natural propension we may have to imagine that simplicity and identity. The comparison of the theatre must not mislead us. They are the successive perceptions only that constitute the mind; nor have we the most distant notion of the place where these scenes are represented, or of the materials of which it is composed.

"What then gives so great a propension to ascribe an identity to these successive perceptions, and to suppose ourselves possessed of an invariable and uninterrupted existence through the whole course of our lives? In order to answer this question, we must distinguish between personal identity as it regards our thought and imagination, and as it regards our passions, or the concern we take in ourselves. The first is our present subject; and to explain it perfectly we must take the matter pretty deep, and account for that identity which we attribute to plants and animals; there being a great analogy betwixt it and the identity of a self or person."--(I. pp. 321, 322.)

Perfect identity is exhibited by an object which remains unchanged throughout a certain time; perfect diversity is seen in two or more objects which are separated by intervals of space and periods of time. But, in both these cases, there is no sharp line of demarcation between identity and diversity, and it is impossible to say when an object ceases to be one and becomes two.

When a sea-anemone multiplies by division, there is a time during which it is said to be one animal partially divided; but, after a while, it becomes two animals adherent together, and the limit between these conditions is purely arbitrary. So in mineralogy, a crystal of a definite chemical composition may have its substance replaced, particle by particle, by another chemical compound. When does it lose its primitive identity and become a new thing?

Again, a plant or an animal, in the course of its existence, from the condition of an egg or seed to the end of life, remains the same neither in form, nor in structure, nor in the matter of which it is composed: every attribute it possesses is constantly changing, and yet we say that it is always one and the same individual. And if, in this case, we attribute identity without supposing an indivisible immaterial something to underlie and condition that identity, why should we need the supposition in the case of that succession of changeful phenomena we call the mind?

In fact, we ascribe identity to an individual plant or animal, simply because there has been no moment of time at which we could observe any division of it Into parts separated by time or space. Every experience we have of it is as one thing and not as two; and we sum up our experiences in the ascription of identity, although we know quite well that, strictly speaking, it has not been the same for any two moments.

So with the mind. Our perceptions flow in even succession; the impressions of the present moment are inextricably mixed up with the memories of yesterday and the expectations of to-morrow, and all are connected by the links of cause and effect.

" ... as the same individual republic may not only change its members, but also its laws and constitutions; in like manner the same person may vary his character and disposition, as well as his impressions and ideas, without losing his identity. Whatever changes he endures, his several parts are still connected by the relation of causation. And in this view our identity with regard to the passions serves to corroborate that with regard to the imagination, by the making our distant perceptions influence each other, and by giving us a present concern for our past or future pains or pleasures.

"As memory alone acquaints us with the continuance and extent of this succession of perceptions, 'tis to be considered, upon that account chiefly, as the source of personal identity. Had we no memory we never should have any notion of causation, nor consequently of that chain of causes and effects which constitute our self or person. But having once acquired this notion of causation from the memory, we can extend the same chain of causes, and consequently the identity of our persons, beyond our memory, and can comprehend times, and circumstances, and actions, which we have entirely forgot, but suppose in general to have existed. For how few of our past actions are there of which we have any memory? Who can tell me, for instance, what were his thoughts and actions on the first of January, 1715, the eleventh of March, 1719, and the third of August, 1733? Or will he affirm, because he has entirely forgot the incidents of those days, that the present self is not the same person with the self of that time, and by that means overturn all the most established notions of personal identity? In this view, therefore, memory does not so much produce as discover personal identity, by showing us the relation of cause and effect among our different perceptions. 'Twill be incumbent on those who affirm that memory produces entirely our personal identity, to give a reason why we can thus extend our identity beyond our memory.

"The whole of this doctrine leads us to a conclusion which is of great importance in the present affair, viz. that all the nice and subtle questions concerning personal identity can never possibly be decided, and are to be regarded rather as grammatical than as philosophical difficulties. Identity depends on the relations of ideas, and these relations produce identity by means of that easy transition they occasion. But as the relations, and the easiness of the transition may diminish by insensible degrees, we have no just standard by which we can decide any dispute concerning the time when they acquire or lose a title to the name of identity. All the disputes concerning the identity of connected objects are merely verbal, except so far as the relation of parts gives rise to some fiction or imaginary principle of union, as we have already observed.

"What I have said concerning the first origin and uncertainty of our notion of identity, as applied to the human mind may be extended, with little or no variation, to that of simplicity. An object, whose different co-existent parts are bound together by a close relation, operates upon the imagination after much the same manner as one perfectly simple and undivisible, and requires not a much greater stretch of thought in order to its conception. From this similarity of operation we attribute a simplicity to it, and feign a principle of union as the support of this simplicity, and the centre of all the different parts and qualities of the object."--(I. pp. 331-3.)

The final result of Hume's reasoning comes to this: As we use the name of body for the sum of the phenomena which make up our corporeal existence, so we employ the name of soul for the sum of the phenomena which constitute our mental existence; and we have no more reason, in the latter case, than in the former, to suppose that there is anything beyond the phenomena which answers to the name. In the case of the soul, as in that of the body, the idea of substance is a mere fiction of the imagination. This conclusion is nothing but a rigorous application of Berkeley's reasoning concerning matter to mind, and it is fully adopted by Kant.[35]

Having arrived at the conclusion that the conception of a soul, as a substantive thing, is a mere figment of the imagination; and that, whether it exists or not, we can by no possibility know anything about it, the inquiry as to the durability of the soul may seem superfluous.

Nevertheless, there is still a sense in which, even under these conditions, such an inquiry is justifiable. Leaving aside the problem of the substance of the soul, and taking the word "soul" simply as a name for the series of mental phenomena which make up an individual mind; it remains open to us to ask, whether that series commenced with, or before, the series of phenomena which constitute the corresponding individual body; and whether it terminates with the end of the corporeal series, or goes on after the existence of the body has ended. And, in both cases, there arises the further question, whether the excess of duration of the mental series over that of the body, is finite or infinite.

Hume has discussed some of these questions in the remarkable essay On the Immortality of the Soul, which was not published till after his death, and which seems long to have remained but little known. Nevertheless, indeed, possibly, for that reason, its influence has been manifested in unexpected quarters, and its main arguments have been adduced by archiepiscopal and episcopal authority in evidence of the value of revelation. Dr. Whately,[36] sometime Archbishop of Dublin, paraphrases Hume, though he forgets to cite him; and Bishop Courtenay's elaborate work,[37] dedicated to the Archbishop, is a development of that prelate's version of Hume's essay.

This little paper occupies only some ten pages, but it is not wonderful that it attracted an acute logician like Whately, for it is a model of clear and vigorous statement. The argument hardly admits of condensation, so that I must let Hume speak for himself:--

"By the mere light of reason it seems difficult to prove the immortality of the soul: the arguments for it are commonly derived either from metaphysical topics, or moral, or physical. But in reality it is the gospel, and the gospel alone, that has brought life and immortality to light.[38]

"1. Metaphysical topics suppose that the soul is immaterial, and that 'tis impossible for thought to belong to a material substance.[39] But just metaphysics teach us that the notion of substance is wholly confused and imperfect; and that we have no other idea of any substance, than as an aggregate of particular qualities inhering in an unknown something. Matter, therefore, and spirit, are at bottom equally unknown, and we cannot determine what qualities inhere in the one or in the other.[40] They likewise teach us, that nothing can be decided a priori concerning any cause or effect; and that experience, being the only source of our judgments of this nature, we cannot know from any other principle, whether matter, by its structure or arrangement, may not be the cause of thought. Abstract reasonings cannot decide any question of fact or existence. But admitting a spiritual substance to be dispersed throughout the universe, like the ethereal fire of the Stoics, and to be the only inherent subject of thought, we have reason to conclude from analogy, that nature uses it after the manner she does the other substance, matter. She employs it as a kind of paste or clay; modifies it into a variety of forms or existences; dissolves after a time each modification, and from its substance erects a new form. As the same material substance may successively compose the bodies of all animals, the same spiritual substance may compose their minds: Their consciousness, or that system of thought which they formed during life, may be continually dissolved by death, and nothing interests them in the new modification. The most positive assertors of the mortality of the soul never denied the immortality of its substance; and that an immaterial substance, as well as a material, may lose its memory or consciousness, appears in part from experience, if the soul be immaterial. Seasoning from the common course of nature, and without supposing any new interposition of the Supreme Cause, which ought always to be excluded from philosophy, what is incorruptible must also be ingenerable. The soul, therefore, if immortal, existed before our birth, and if the former existence noways concerned us, neither will the latter. Animals undoubtedly feel, think, love, hate, will, and even reason, though in a more imperfect manner than men: Are their souls also immaterial and immortal?"[41]

Hume next proceeds to consider the moral arguments, and chiefly

" ... those derived from the justice of God, which is supposed to be further interested in the future punishment of the vicious and reward of the virtuous."

But if by the justice of God we moan the same attribute which we call justice in ourselves, then why should either reward or punishment be extended beyond this life?[42] Our sole means of knowing anything is the reasoning faculty which God has given us; and that reasoning faculty not only denies us any conception of a future state, but fails to furnish a single valid argument in favour of the belief that the mind will endure after the dissolution of the body.

" ... If any purpose of nature be clear, we may affirm that the whole scope and intention of man's creation, so far as we can judge by natural reason, is limited to the present life."

To the argument that the powers of man are so much greater than the needs of this life require, that they suggest a future scene in which they can be employed, Hume replies:--

"If the reason of man gives him great superiority above other animals, his necessities are proportionably multiplied upon him; his whole time, his whole capacity, activity, courage, and passion, find sufficient employment in fencing against the miseries of his present condition; and frequently, nay, almost always, are too slender for the business assigned them. A pair of shoes, perhaps, was never yet wrought to the highest degree of perfection that commodity is capable of attaining; yet it is necessary, at least very useful, that there should be some politicians and moralists, even some geometers, poets and philosophers, among mankind. The powers of men are no more superior to their wants, considered merely in this life, than those of foxes and hares are, compared to their wants and to their period of existence. The inference from parity of reason is therefore obvious."

In short, Hume argues that, if the faculties with which we are endowed are unable to discover a future state, and if the most attentive consideration of their nature serves to show that they are adapted to this life and nothing more, it is surely inconsistent with any conception of justice that we should be dealt with, as if we had all along had a clear knowledge of the fact thus carefully concealed from us. What should we think of the justice of a father, who gave his son every reason to suppose that a trivial fault would only be visited by a box on the ear; and then, years afterwards, put him on the rack for a week for the same fault?

Again, the suggestion arises, if God is the cause of all things, he is responsible for evil as well as for good; and it appears utterly irreconcilable with our notions of justice that he should punish another for that which he has, in fact, done himself. Moreover, just punishment bears a proportion to the offence, while suffering which is infinite is ipso facto disproportionate to any finite deed.

"Why then eternal punishment for the temporary offences of so frail a creature as man? Can any one approve of Alexander's rage, who intended to exterminate a whole nation because they had seized his favourite horse Bucephalus?

"Heaven and hell suppose two distinct species of men, the good and the bad; but the greatest part of mankind float betwixt vice and virtue. Were one to go round the world with the intention of giving a good supper to the righteous and a sound drubbing to the wicked, he would frequently be embarrassed in his choice, and would find the merits and demerits of most men and women scarcely amount to the value of either."[43]

One can but admire the broad humanity and the insight into the springs of action manifest in this passage. Comprendre est ?moiti?pardonner. The more one knows of the real conditions which determine men's acts the less one finds either to praise or blame. For kindly David Hume, "the damnation of one man is an infinitely greater evil in the universe than the subversion of a thousand million of kingdoms." And he would have felt with his countryman Burns, that even "auld Nickie Ben" should "hae a chance."

As against those who reason for the necessity of a future state, in order that the justice of the Deity may be satisfied, Hume's argumentation appears unanswerable. For if the justice of God resembles what we mean by justice, the bestowal of infinite happiness for finite well-doing and infinite misery for finite ill-doing, it is in no sense just. And, if the justice of God does not resemble what we mean by justice, it is an abuse of language to employ the name of justice for the attribute described by it. But, as against those who choose to argue that there is nothing in what is known to us of the attributes of the Deity inconsistent with a future state of rewards and punishments, Hume's pleadings have no force. Bishop Butler's argument that, inasmuch as the visitation of our acts by rewards and punishments takes place in this life, rewards and punishments must be consistent with the attributes of the Deity, and therefore may go on as long as the mind endures, is unanswerable. Whatever exists is, by the hypothesis, existent by the will of God; and, therefore, the pains and pleasures which exist now may go on existing for all eternity, either increasing, diminishing, or being endlessly varied in their intensity, as they are now.

It is remarkable that Hume does not refer to the sentimental arguments for the immortality of the soul which are so much in vogue at the present day;

and which are based upon our desire for a longer conscious existence than that which nature appears to have allotted to us. Perhaps he did not think them worth notice. For indeed it is not a little strange, that our strong desire that a certain occurrence should happen should be put forward as evidence that it will happen. If my intense desire to see the friend, from whom I have parted, does not bring him from the other side of the world, or take me thither; if the mother's agonised prayer that her child should live has not prevented him from dying; experience certainly affords no presumption that the strong desire to be alive after death, which we call the aspiration after immortality, is any more likely to be gratified. As Hume truly says, "All doctrines are to be suspected which are favoured by our passions;" and the doctrine, that we are immortal because we should extremely like to be so, contains the quintessence of suspiciousness.

In respect of the existence and attributes of the soul, as of those of the Deity, then, logic is powerless and reason silent. At the most we can get no further than the conclusion of Kant:--

"After we have satisfied ourselves of the vanity of all the ambitious attempts of reason to fly beyond the bounds of experience, enough remains of practical value to content us. It is true that no one may boast that he knows that God and a future life exist; for, if he possesses such knowledge, he is just the man for whom I have long been seeking. All knowledge (touching an object of mere reason) can be communicated, and therefore I might hope to see my own knowledge increased to this prodigious extent, by his instruction. No; our conviction in these matters is not logical, but moral certainty; and, inasmuch as it rests upon subjective grounds, (of moral disposition) I must not even say: it is morally certain that there is a God, and so on; but, I am morally certain, and so on. That is to say: the belief in a God and in another world is so interwoven with my moral nature, that the former can no more vanish, than the latter can ever be torn from me.

"The only point to be remarked here is that this act of faith of the intellect (Vernunftglaube) assumes the existence of moral dispositions. If we leave them aside, and suppose a mind quite indifferent to moral laws, the inquiry started by reason becomes merely a subject for speculation; and [the conclusion attained] may then indeed be supported by strong arguments from analogy, but not by such as are competent to overcome persistent scepticism.

"There is no one, however, who can fail to be interested in these questions. For, although he may be excluded from moral influences by the want of a good disposition, yet, even in this case, enough remains to lead him to fear a divine existence and a future state. To this end, no more is necessary than that he can at least have no certainty that there is no such being, and no future life; for, to make this conclusion demonstratively certain, he must be able to prove the impossibility of both; and this assuredly no rational man can undertake to do. This negative belief, indeed, cannot produce either morality or good dispositions, but can operate in an analogous fashion, by powerfully repressing the outbreak of evil tendencies.

"But it will be said, is this all that Pure Reason can do when it gazes out beyond the bounds of experience? Nothing more than two articles of faith? Common sense could achieve as much without calling the philosophers to its counsels!

"I will not here speak of the service which philosophy has rendered to human reason by the laborious efforts of its criticism, granting that the outcome proves to be merely negative: about that matter something is to be said in the following section. But do you then ask, that the knowledge which interests all men shall transcend the common understanding and be discovered for you only by philosophers? The very thing which you make a reproach, is the best confirmation of the justice of the previous conclusions, since it shows that which could not, at first, have been anticipated: namely, that in those matters which concern all men alike, nature is not guilty of distributing her gifts with partiality; and that the highest philosophy, in dealing with the most important concerns of humanity, is able to take us no further than the guidance which she affords to the commonest understanding."[44]

In short, nothing can be proved or disproved, respecting either the distinct existence, the substance, or the durability of the soul. So far, Kant is at one with Hume. But Kant adds, as you cannot disprove the immortality of the soul, and as the belief therein is very useful for moral purposes, you may assume it. To which, had Hume lived half a century later, he would probably have replied, that, if morality has no better foundation than an assumption, it is not likely to bear much strain; and, if it has a better foundation, the assumption rather weakens than strengthens it.

As has been already said, Hume is not content with denying that we know anything about the existence or the nature of the soul; but he carries the war into the enemy's camp, and accuses those who affirm the immateriality, simplicity, and indivisibility of the thinking substance, of atheism and Spinozism, which are assumed to be convertible terms.

The method of attack is ingenious. Observation appears to acquaint us with two different systems of beings, and both Spinoza and orthodox philosophers agree, that the necessary substratum of each of these is a substance, in which the phenomena adhere, or of which they are attributes or modes.

"I observe first the universe of objects or of body; the sun, moon, and stars; the earth, seas, plants, animals, men, ships, houses, and other productions either of art or of nature. Here Spinoza appears, and tells me that these are only modifications and that the subject in which they inhere is simple, uncompounded, and indivisible. After this I consider the other system of beings, viz. the universe of thought, or my impressions and ideas. Then I observe another sun, moon, and stars; an earth and seas, covered and inhabited by plants and animals, towns, houses, mountains, rivers; and, in short, everything I can discover or conceive in the first system. Upon my inquiring concerning these, theologians present themselves, and tell me that these also are modifications, and modifications of one simple, uncompounded, and indivisible substance. Immediately upon which I am deafened with the noise of a hundred voices, that treat the first hypothesis with detestation and scorn, and the second with applause and veneration. I turn my attention to these hypotheses to see what may be the reason of so great a partiality; and find that they have the same fault of being unintelligible, and that, as far as we can understand them, they are so much alike, that 'tis impossible to discover any absurdity in one, which is not common to both of them."--(I. p. 309.)

For the manner in which Hume makes his case good, I must refer to the original. Plain people may rest satisfied that both hypotheses are unintelligible, without plunging any further among syllogisms, the premisses of which convey no meaning, while the conclusions carry no conviction.

FOOTNOTES:

[35] "Our internal intuition shows no permanent existence, for the Ego is only the consciousness of my thinking." "There is no means whatever by which we can learn anything respecting the constitution of the soul, so far as regards the possibility of its separate existence."--Kritik von den Paralogismen der reinen Vernunft.

[36] Essays on Some of the Peculiarities of the Christian Religion, (Essay I. Revelation of a Future State), by Richard Whately, D.D., Archbishop of Dublin. Fifth Edition, revised, 1846.

[37] The Future States: their Evidences and Nature; considered on Principles Physical, Moral, and Scriptural, with the Design of showing the Value of the Gospel Revelation by the Right Rev. Reginald Courtenay, D.D., Lord Bishop of Kingston (Jamaica), 1857.

[38] "Now that 'Jesus Christ brought life and immortality to light through the Gospel,' and that in the most literal sense, which implies that the revelation of the doctrine is peculiar to His Gospel, seems to be at least the most obvious meaning of the Scriptures of the New Testament."--Whately, l.c. p. 27.

[39] Compare, Of the Immateriality of the Soul, Section V. of

Part IV., Book I., of the Treatise, in which Hume concludes (I. p. 319)

that, whether it be material or immaterial, "in both cases the metaphysical arguments for the immortality of the soul are equally inconclusive; and in both cases the moral arguments and those derived from the analogy of nature are equally strong and convincing."

[40] "The question again respecting the materiality of the soul is one which I am at a loss to understand clearly, till it shall have been clearly determined what matter is. We know nothing of it, any more than of mind, except its attributes."--Whately, l.c. p. 66.

[41] "None of those who contend for the natural immortality of the soul ... have been able to extricate themselves from one difficulty, viz. that all their arguments apply, with exactly the same force, to prove an immortality, not only of brutes, but even of plants; though in such a conclusion as this they are never willing to acquiesce."--Whately, l.c. p. 67.

[42] "Nor are we therefore authorised to infer ?priori, independent of Revelation, a future state of retribution, from the irregularities prevailing in the present life, since that future state does not account fully for these irregularities. It may explain, indeed, how present evil may be conducive to future good, but not why the good could not be attained without the evil; it may reconcile with our notions of the divine justice the present prosperity of the wicked, but it does not account for the existence of the wicked."--Whately, l.c. pp. 69, 70.

[43] "So reason also shows, that for man to expect to earn for himself by the practice of virtue, and claim, as his just right, an immortality of exalted happiness, is a most extravagant and groundless pretension."--Whately, l.c. p. 101. On the other hand, however, the Archbishop sees no unreasonableness in a man's earning for himself an immortality of intense unhappiness by the practice of vice. So that life is, naturally, a venture in which you may lose all, but can earn nothing. It may be thought somewhat hard upon mankind if they are pushed into a speculation of this sort, willy-nilly.

[44] Kritik der reinen Vernunft. Ed. Hartenstein, p. 547.

CHAPTER X.

VOLITION: LIBERTY AND NECESSITY.

In the opening paragraphs of the third part of the second book of the Treatise, Hume gives a description of the will.

"Of all the immediate effects of pain and pleasure there is none more remarkable than the will; and though, properly speaking, it be not comprehended among the passions, yet as the full understanding of its nature and properties is necessary to the explanation of them, we shall here make it the subject of our inquiry. I desire it may be observed, that, by the will, I mean nothing but the internal impression we feel, and are conscious of, when we knowingly give rise to any new motion of our body, or new perception of our mind. This impression, like the preceding ones of pride and humility, love and hatred, 'tis impossible to define, and needless to describe any further."--(II. p. 150.)

This description of volition may be criticised on various grounds. More especially does it seem defective in restricting the term "will" to that feeling which arises when we act, or appear to act, as causes: for one may will to strike, without striking; or to think of something which we have forgotten.

Every volition is a complex idea composed of two elements: the one is the idea of an action; the other is a desire for the occurrence of that action. If I will to strike, I have an idea of a certain movement, and a desire that that movement should take place; if I will to think of any subject, or, in other words, to attend to that subject, I have an idea of the subject and a strong desire that it should remain present to my consciousness. And so far as I can discover, this combination of an idea of an object with an emotion, is everything that can be directly observed in an act of volition. So that Hume's definition may be amended thus: Volition is the impression which arises when the idea of a bodily or mental action is accompanied by the desire that the action should be accomplished. It differs from other desires simply in the fact, that we regard ourselves as possible causes of the action desired.

Two questions arise, in connexion with the observation of the phenomenon of volition, as they arise out of the contemplation of all other natural phenomena. Firstly, has it a cause; and, if so, what is its cause? Secondly, is it followed by any effect, and if so, what effect does it produce?

Hume points out, that the nature of the phenomena we consider can have nothing to do with the origin of the conception that they are connected by the relation of cause and effect. For that relation is nothing but an order of succession, which, so far as our experience goes, is invariable; and it is obvious that the nature of phenomena has nothing to do with their order. Whatever it is that leads us to seek for a cause for every event, in the case of the phenomena of the external world, compels us, with equal cogency, to seek it in that of the mind.

The only meaning of the law of causation, in the physical world, is, that it generalises universal experience of the order of that world; and, if experience shows a similar order to obtain among states of consciousness, the law of causation will properly express that order.

That such an order exists, however, is acknowledged by every sane man:

"Our idea, therefore, of necessity and causation, arises entirely from the uniformity observable in the operations of nature, where similar objects are constantly conjoined together, and the mind is determined by custom to infer the one from the appearance of the other. These two circumstances form the whole of that necessity which we ascribe to matter. Beyond the constant conjunction of similar objects and the consequent inference from one to the other, we have no notion of any necessity of connexion.

"If it appear, therefore, what all mankind have ever allowed, without any doubt or hesitation, that these two circumstances take place in the voluntary actions of men, and in the operations of mind, it must follow that all mankind have ever agreed in the doctrine of necessity, and that they have hitherto disputed merely from not understanding each other."--(IV. p. 97.)

But is this constant conjunction observable in human actions? A student of history could give but one answer to this question:

"Ambition, avarice, self-love, vanity, friendship, generosity, public spirit: these passions, mixed in various degrees, and distributed through society, have been, from the beginning of the world, and still are, the source of all the actions and enterprizes which have ever been observed among mankind. Would you know the sentiments, inclinations, and course of life of the Greeks and Romans? Study well the temper and actions of the French and English. You cannot be much mistaken in transferring to the former most of the observations which you have made with regard to the latter. Mankind are so much the same, in all times and places, that history informs us of nothing new or strange in this particular. Its chief use is only to discover the constant and universal principles of human nature, by showing men in all varieties of circumstances and situations, and furnishing us with materials from which we may form our observations, and become acquainted with the regular springs of human action and behaviour. These records of wars, intrigues, factions, and revolutions are so many collections of experiments, by which the politician or moral philosopher fixes the principles of his science, in the same manner as the physician or natural philosopher becomes acquainted with the nature of plants, minerals, and other external objects, by the experiments which he forms concerning them. Nor are the earth, air, water, and other elements examined by Aristotle and Hippocrates more like to those which at present lie under our observation, than the men described by Polybius and Tacitus are to those who now govern the world."--(IV. pp. 97-8.)

Hume proceeds to point out that the value set upon experience in the conduct of affairs, whether of business or of politics, involves the acknowledgment that we base our expectation of what men will do, upon our observation of what they have done; and, that we are as firmly convinced of the fixed order of thoughts as we are of that of things. And, if it be urged that human actions not unfrequently appear unaccountable and capricious, his reply is prompt:--

"I grant it possible to find some actions which seem to have no regular connexion with any known motives, and are exceptions to all the measures of conduct which have ever been established for the government of men. But if one could willingly know what judgment should be formed of such irregular and extraordinary actions, we may consider the sentiments commonly entertained with regard to those irregular events which appear in the course of nature, and the operations of external objects. All causes are not conjoined to their usual effects with like uniformity. An artificer, who handles only dead matter, may be disappointed in his aim, as well as the politician who directs the conduct of sensible and intelligent agents.

"The vulgar, who take things according to their first appearance, attribute the uncertainty of events to such an uncertainty in the causes as make the latter often fail of their usual influence, though they meet with no impediment to their operation. But philosophers, observing that, almost in every part of nature, there is contained a vast variety of springs and principles, which are hid, by reason of their minuteness or remoteness, find that it is at least possible the contrariety of events may not proceed from any contingency in the cause, but from the secret operation of contrary causes. This possibility is converted into certainty by further observation, when they remark that, upon an exact scrutiny, a contrariety of effects always betrays a contrariety of causes, and proceeds from their mutual opposition. A peasant can give no better reason for the stopping of any clock or watch, than to say that it does not commonly go right. But an artist easily perceives that the same force in the spring or pendulum has always the same influence on the wheels; but fails of its usual effect, perhaps by reason of a grain of dust, which puts a stop to the whole movement. From the observation of several parallel instances, philosophers form a maxim, that the connexion between all causes and effects is equally necessary, and that its seeming uncertainty in some instances proceeds from the secret opposition of contrary causes."--(IV. pp. 101-2.)

So with regard to human actions:--

"The internal principles and motives may operate in a uniform manner, notwithstanding these seeming irregularities; in the same manner as the winds, rains, clouds, and other variations of the weather are supposed to be governed by steady principles; though not easily discoverable by human sagacity and inquiry."--(IV. p. 103.)

Meteorology, as a science, was not in existence in Hume's time, or he would have left out the "supposed to be." In practice, again, what difference does any one make between natural and moral evidence?

"A prisoner who has neither money nor interest, discovers the impossibility of his escape, as well when he considers the obstinacy of the gaoler, as the walls and bars with which he is surrounded; and, in all attempts for his freedom, chooses rather to work upon the stone and iron of the one, than upon the inflexible nature of the other. The same prisoner, when conducted to the scaffold, foresees his death as certainly from the constancy and fidelity of his guards, as from the operation of the axe or wheel. His mind runs along a certain train of ideas: The refusal of the soldiers to consent to his escape; the action of the executioner; the separation of the head and body; bleeding, convulsive motions, and death. Here is a connected chain of natural causes and voluntary actions; but the mind feels no difference between them, in passing from one link to another, nor is less certain of the future event, than if it were connected with the objects presented to the memory or senses, by a train of causes cemented together by what we are pleased to call a physical necessity. The same experienced union has the same effect on the mind, whether the united objects be motives, volition, and actions; or figure and motion. We may change the names of things, but their nature and their operation on the understanding never change."--(IV. pp. 105-6.)

But, if the necessary connexion of our acts with our ideas has always been acknowledged in practice, why the proclivity of mankind to deny it words?

"If we examine the operations of body, and the production of effects from their causes, we shall find that all our faculties can never carry us further in our knowledge of this relation, than barely to observe, that particular objects are constantly conjoined together, and that the mind is carried, by a customary transition, from the appearance of the one to the belief of the other. But though this conclusion concerning human ignorance be the result of the strictest scrutiny of this subject, men still entertain a strong propensity to believe, that they penetrate further into the province of nature, and perceive something like a necessary connexion between cause and effect. When, again, they turn their reflections towards the operations of their own minds, and feel no such connexion between the motive and the action; they are thence apt to suppose, that there is a difference between the effects which result from material force, and those which arise from thought and intelligence. But, being once convinced, that we know nothing of causation of any kind, than merely the constant conjunction of objects, and the consequent inference of the mind from one to another, and finding that these two circumstances are universally allowed to have place in voluntary actions; we may be more easily led to own the same necessity common to all causes."--(IV. pp. 107, 8.)

The last asylum of the hard-pressed advocate of the doctrine of uncaused volition is usually, that, argue as you like, he has a profound and ineradicable consciousness of what he calls the freedom of his will. But Hume follows him even here, though only in a note, as if he thought the extinction of so transparent a sophism hardly worthy of the dignity of his text.

"The prevalence of the doctrine of liberty may be accounted for from another cause, viz. a false sensation, or seeming experience, which we have, or may have, of liberty or indifference in many of our actions. The necessity of any action, whether of matter or of mind, is not, properly speaking, a quality in the agent, but in any thinking or intelligent being who may consider the action; and it consists chiefly in the determination of his thoughts to infer the existence of that action from some preceding objects; as liberty, when opposed to necessity, is nothing but the want of that determination, and a certain looseness or indifference which we feel, in passing or not passing, from the idea of any object to the idea of any succeeding one. Now we may observe that though, in reflecting on human actions, we seldom feel such looseness or indifference, but are commonly able to infer them with considerable certainty from their motives, and from the dispositions of the agent; yet it frequently happens, that in performing the actions themselves, we are sensible of something like it: And as all resembling objects are taken for each other, this has been employed as demonstrative and even intuitive proof of human liberty. We feel that our actions are subject to our will on most occasions; and imagine we feel, that the will itself is subject to nothing, because, when by a denial of it we are provoked to try, we feel that it moves easily every way, and produces an image of itself (or a Velleity as it is called in the schools), even on that side on which it did not settle. This image or faint notion, we persuade ourselves, could at that time have been completed into the thing itself; because, should that be denied, we find upon a second trial that at present it can. We consider not that the fantastical desire of showing liberty is here the motive of our actions."--(IV. p. 110, note.)

Moreover, the moment the attempt is made to give a definite meaning to the words, the supposed opposition between free will and necessity turns out to be a mere verbal dispute.

"For what is meant by liberty, when applied to voluntary actions? We cannot surely mean, that actions have so little connexion with motive, inclinations, and circumstances, that one does not follow with a certain degree of uniformity from the other, and that one affords no inference by which we can conclude the existence of the other. For these are plain and acknowledged matters of fact. By liberty, then, we can only mean a power of acting or not acting according to the determinations of the will; that is, if we choose to remain at rest, we may; if we choose to move, we also may. Now this hypothetical liberty is universally allowed to belong to every one who is not a prisoner and in chains. Here then is no subject of dispute."--(IV. p. 111.)

Half the controversies about the freedom of the will would have had no existence, if this pithy paragraph had been well pondered by those who oppose the doctrine of necessity. For they rest upon the absurd presumption that the proposition, "I can do as I like," is contradictory to the doctrine of necessity. The answer is; nobody doubts that, at any rate within certain limits, you can do as you like. But what determines your likings and dislikings? Did you make your own constitution? Is it your contrivance that one thing is pleasant and another is painful? And even if it were, why did you prefer to make it after the one fashion rather than the other? The passionate assertion of the consciousness of their freedom, which is the favourite refuge of the opponents of the doctrine of necessity, is mere futility, for nobody denies it. What they really have to do, if they would upset the necessarian argument, is to prove that they are free to associate any emotion whatever with any idea whatever; to like pain as much as pleasure; vice as much as virtue; in short, to prove, that, whatever may be the fixity of order of the universe of things, that of thought is given over to chance.

In the second part of this remarkable essay, Hume considers the real, or supposed, immoral consequences of the doctrine of necessity, premising the weighty observation that

"When any opinion leads to absurdity, it is certainly false; but it is not certain that an opinion is false because it is of dangerous consequence."--(IV. p. 112.)

And, therefore, that the attempt to refute an opinion by a picture of its dangerous consequences to religion and morality, is as illogical as it is reprehensible.

It is said, in the first place, that necessity destroys responsibility; that, as it is usually put, we have no right to praise or blame actions that cannot be helped. Hume's reply amounts to this, that the very idea of responsibility implies the belief in the necessary connexion of certain actions with certain states of the mind. A person is held responsible only for those acts which are preceded by a certain intention; and, as we cannot see, or hear, or feel, an intention, we can only reason out its existence on the principle that like effects have like causes.

If a man is found by the police busy with "jemmy" and dark lantern at a jeweller's shop door over night, the magistrate before whom he is brought the next morning, reasons from those effects to their causes in the fellow's "burglarious" ideas and volitions, with perfect confidence, and punishes him accordingly. And it is quite clear that such a proceeding would be grossly unjust, if the links of the logical process were other than necessarily connected together. The advocate who should attempt to get the man off on the plea that his client need not necessarily have had a felonious intent, would hardly waste his time more, if he tried to prove that the sum of all the angles of a triangle is not two right angles, but three.

A man's moral responsibility for his acts has, in fact, nothing to do with the causation of these acts, but depends on the frame of mind which accompanies them. Common language tells us this, when it uses "well-disposed" as the equivalent of "good," and "evil-minded" as that of "wicked." If A does something which puts B in a violent passion, it is quite possible to admit that B's passion is the necessary consequence of A's act, and yet to believe that B's fury is morally wrong, or that he ought to control it. In fact, a calm bystander would reason with both on the assumption of moral necessity. He would say to A, "You were wrong in doing a thing which you knew (that is, of the necessity of which you were convinced) would irritate B." And he would say to B, "You are wrong to give way to passion, for you know its evil effects"--that is the necessary connection between yielding to passion and evil.

So far, therefore, from necessity destroying moral responsibility, it is the foundation of all praise and blame; and moral admiration reaches its climax in the ascription of necessary goodness to the Deity.

To the statement of another consequence of the necessarian doctrine, that, if there be a God, he must be the cause of all evil as well as of all good, Hume gives no real reply--probably because none is possible. But then, if this conclusion is distinctly and unquestionably deducible from the doctrine of necessity, it is no less unquestionably a direct consequence of every known form of monotheism. If God is the cause of all things, he must be the cause of evil among the rest; if he is omniscient, he must have the fore-knowledge of evil; if he is almighty, he must possess the power of preventing, or of extinguishing evil. And to say that an all-knowing and all-powerful being is not responsible for what happens, because he only permits it, is, under its intellectual aspect, a piece of childish sophistry; while, as to the moral look of it, one has only to ask any decently honourable man, whether, under like circumstances, he would try to get rid of his responsibility by such a plea.

Hume's Inquiry appeared in 1748. He does not refer to Anthony Collins' essay on Liberty, published thirty-three years before, in which the same question is treated to the same effect, with singular force and lucidity. It may be said, perhaps, that it is not wonderful that the two freethinkers should follow the same line of reasoning; but no such theory will account for the fact that in 1754, the famous Calvinistic divine, Jonathan Edwards, President of the College of New Jersey, produced, in the interests of the straitest orthodoxy, a demonstration of the necessarian thesis, which has never been equalled in power, and certainly has never been refuted.

In the ninth section of the fourth part of Edwards' Inquiry, he has to deal with the Arminian objection to the Calvinistic doctrine that "it makes God the author of sin"; and it is curious to watch the struggle between the theological controversialist, striving to ward off an admission which he knows will be employed to damage his side, and the acute logician, conscious that, in some shape or other, the admission must be made. Beginning with a tu quoque, that the Arminian doctrine involves consequences as bad as the Calvinistic view, he proceeds to object to the term "author of sin," though he ends by admitting that, in a certain sense, it is applicable; he proves from Scripture, that God is the disposer and orderer of sin; and then, by an elaborate false analogy with the darkness resulting from the absence of the sun, endeavours to suggest that he is only the author of it in a negative sense; and, finally, he takes refuge in the conclusion that, though God is the orderer and disposer of those deeds which, considered in relation to their agents, are morally evil, yet, inasmuch as His purpose has all along been infinitely good, they are not evil relatively to him.

And this, of course, may be perfectly true; but if true, it is inconsistent with the attribute of omnipotence. It is conceivable that there should be no evil in the world; that which is conceivable is certainly possible; if it were possible for evil to be non-existent, the maker of the world, who, though foreknowing the existence of evil in that world, did not prevent it, either did not really desire it should not exist, or could not prevent its existence. It might be well for those who inveigh against the logical consequences of necessarianism to bethink them of the logical consequences of theism; which are not only the same, when the attribute of Omniscience is ascribed to the Deity, but which bring out, from the existence of moral evil, a hopeless conflict between the attributes of Infinite Benevolence and Infinite Power, which, with no less assurance, are affirmed to appertain to the Divine Being.

Kant's mode of dealing with the doctrine of necessity is very singular. That the phenomena of the mind follow fixed relations of cause and effect is, to him, as unquestionable as it is to Hume. But then there is the Ding an sich, the Noumenon, or Kantian equivalent for the substance of the soul. This, being out of the phenomenal world, is subject to none of the laws of phenomena, and is consequently as absolutely free, and as completely powerless, as a mathematical point, in vacua, would be. Hence volition is uncaused, so far as it belongs to the noumenon; but, necessary, so far as it takes effect in the phenomenal world.

Since Kant is never weary of telling us that we know nothing whatever, and can know nothing, about the noumenon, except as the hypothetical subject of any number of negative predicates; the information that it is free, in the sense of being out of reach of the law of causation, is about as valuable as the assertion that it is neither grey, nor blue, nor square. For practical purposes, it must be admitted that the inward possession of such a noumenal libertine does not amount to much for people whose actual existence is made up of nothing but definitely regulated phenomena. When the good and evil angels fought for the dead body of Moses, its presence must have been of about the same value to either of the contending parties, as that of Kant's noumenon, in the battle of impulses which rages in the breast of man. Metaphysicians, as a rule, are sadly deficient in the sense of humour; or they would surely abstain from advancing propositions which, when stripped of the verbiage in which they are disguised, appear to the profane eye to be bare shams, naked but not ashamed.

CHAPTER XI.

THE PRINCIPLES OF MORALS.

In his autobiography, Hume writes:--

"In the same year [1752] was published at London my Inquiry Concerning the Principles of Morals; which in my own opinion (who ought not to judge on that subject) is of all my writings, historical, philosophical, and literary, incomparably the best. It came unnoticed and unobserved into the world."

It may commonly be noticed that the relative value which an author ascribes to his own works rarely agrees with the estimate formed of them by his readers; who criticise the products, without either the power or the wish to take into account the pains which they may have cost the producer. Moreover, the clear and dispassionate common sense of the Inquiry concerning the Principles of Morals may have tasted flat after the highly-seasoned Inquiry concerning the Human Understanding. Whether the public like to be deceived, or not, may be open to question; but it is beyond a doubt that they love to be shocked in a pleasant and mannerly way. Now Hume's speculations on moral questions are not so remote from those of respectable professors, like Hutcheson, or saintly prelates, such as Butler, as to present any striking novelty. And they support the cause of righteousness in a cool, reasonable, indeed slightly patronising fashion, eminently in harmony with the mind of the eighteenth century; which admired virtue very much, if she would only avoid the rigour which the age called fanaticism, and the fervour which it called enthusiasm.

Having applied the ordinary methods of scientific inquiry to the intellectual phenomena of the mind, it was natural that Hume should extend the same mode of investigation to its moral phenomena; and, in the true spirit of a natural philosopher, he commences by selecting a group of those states of consciousness with which every one's personal experience must have made him familiar: in the expectation that the discovery of the sources of moral approbation and disapprobation, in this comparatively easy case, may furnish the means of detecting them where they are more recondite.

"We shall analyse that complication of mental qualities which form what, in common life, we call PERSONAL MERIT: We shall consider every attribute of the mind, which renders a man an object either of esteem and affection, or of hatred and contempt; every habit or sentiment or faculty, which if ascribed to any person, implies either praise or blame, and may enter into any panegyric or satire of his character and manners. The quick sensibility which, on this head, is so universal among mankind, gives a philosopher sufficient assurance that he can never be considerably mistaken in framing the catalogue, or incurs any danger of misplacing the objects of his contemplation: He needs only enter into his own breast for a moment, and consider whether he should or should not desire to have this or that quality assigned to him, and whether such or such an imputation would proceed from a friend or an enemy. The very nature of language guides us almost infallibly in forming a judgment of this nature; and as every tongue possesses one set of words which are taken in a good sense, and another in the opposite, the least acquaintance with the idiom suffices, without any reasoning, to direct us in collecting and arranging the estimable or blamable qualities of men. The only object of reasoning is to discover the circumstances on both sides, which are common to these qualities; to observe that particular in which the estimable qualities agree on the one hand, and the blamable on the other, and thence to reach the foundation of ethics, and find their universal principles, from which all censure or approbation is ultimately derived. As this is a question of fact, not of abstract science, we can only expect success by following the experimental method, and deducing general maxims from a comparison of particular instances. The other scientifical method, where a general abstract principle is first established, and is afterwards branched out into a variety of inferences and conclusions, may be more perfect in itself, but suits less the imperfection of human nature, and is a common source of illusion and mistake, in this as well as in other subjects. Men are now cured of their passion for hypotheses and systems in natural philosophy, and will hearken to no arguments but those which are derived from experience. It is full time they should attempt a like reformation in all moral disquisitions; and reject every system of ethics, however subtile or ingenious, which is not founded on fact and observation."--(IV. pp. 242-4.)

No qualities give a man a greater claim to personal merit than benevolence and justice; but if we inquire why benevolence deserves so much praise, the answer will certainly contain a large reference to the utility of that virtue to society; and as for justice, the very existence of the virtue implies that of society; public utility is its sole origin; and the measure of its usefulness is also the standard of its merit. If every man possessed everything he wanted, and no one had the power to interfere with such possession; or if no man desired that which could damage his fellow-man, justice would have no part to play in the universe. But as Hume observes:--

"In the present disposition of the human heart, it would perhaps be difficult to find complete instances of such enlarged affections; but still we may observe that the case of families approaches towards it; and the stronger the mutual benevolence is among the individuals, the nearer it approaches, till all distinction of property be in a great measure lost and confounded among them. Between married persons, the cement of friendship is by the laws supposed so strong, as to abolish all division of possessions, and has often, in reality, the force assigned to it.[45] And it is observable that, during the ardour of new enthusiasms, when every principle is inflamed into extravagance, the community of goods has frequently been attempted; and nothing but experience of its inconveniences, from the returning or disguised selfishness of men, could make the imprudent fanatics adopt anew the ideas of justice and separate property. So true is it that this virtue derives its existence entirely from its necessary use to the intercourse and social state of mankind."--(IV. p. 256.)

"Were the human species so framed by nature as that each individual possessed within himself every faculty requisite both for his own preservation and for the propagation of his kind: Were all society and intercourse cut off between man and man by the primary intention of the Supreme Creator: It seems evident that so solitary a being would be as much incapable of justice as of social discourse and conversation. Where mutual regard and forbearance serve to no manner of purpose, they would never direct the conduct of any reasonable man. The headlong course of the passions would be checked by no reflection on future consequences. And as each man is here supposed to love himself alone, and to depend only on himself and his own activity for safety and happiness, he would, on every occasion, to the utmost of his power, challenge the preference above every other being, to none of which he is bound by any ties, either of nature or of interest.

"But suppose the conjunction of the sexes to be established in nature, a family immediately arises; and particular rules being found requisite for its subsistence, these are immediately embraced, though without comprehending the rest of mankind within their prescriptions. Suppose that several families unite together in one society, which is totally disjoined from all others, the rules which preserve peace and order enlarge themselves to the utmost extent of that society; but becoming then entirely useless, lose their force when carried one step further. But again, suppose that several distinct societies maintain a kind of intercourse for mutual convenience and advantage, the boundaries of justice still grow larger, in proportion to the largeness of men's views and the force of their mutual connexion. History, experience, reason, sufficiently instruct us in this natural progress of human sentiments, and in the gradual enlargement of our regard to justice in proportion as we become acquainted with the extensive utility of that virtue."--(IV. pp. 262-4.)

The moral obligation of justice and the rights of property are by no means diminished by this exposure of the purely utilitarian basis on which they rest:- -

"For what stronger foundation can be desired or conceived for any duty, than to observe that human society, or even human nature, could not subsist without the establishment of it, and will still arrive at greater degrees of happiness and perfection, the more inviolable the regard is which is paid to that duty?

"The dilemma seems obvious: As justice evidently tends to promote public utility, and to support civil society, the sentiment of justice is either derived from our reflecting on that tendency, or, like hunger, thirst, and other appetites, resentment, love of life, attachment to offspring, and other passions, arises from a simple original instinct in the human heart, which nature has implanted for like salutary purposes. If the latter be the case, it follows that property, which is the object of justice, is also distinguished by a simple original instinct, and is not ascertained by any argument or reflection. But who is there that ever heard of such an instinct? Or is this a subject in which new discoveries can be made? We may as well expect to discover in the body new senses which had before escaped the observation of all mankind."--(IV. pp. 273, 4.)

The restriction of the object of justice to property, in this passage, is singular. Pleasure and pain can hardly be included under the term property, and yet justice surely deals largely with the withholding of the former, or the infliction of the latter, by men on one another. If a man bars another from a pleasure which he would otherwise enjoy, or actively hurts him without good reason, the latter is said to be injured as much as if his property had been interfered with. Here, indeed, it may be readily shown, that it is as much the interest of society that men should not interfere with one another's freedom, or mutually inflict positive or negative pain, as that they should not meddle with one another's property; and hence the obligation of justice in such matters may be deduced. But, if a man merely thinks ill of another, or feels maliciously towards him without due cause, he is properly said to be unjust. In this case it would be hard to prove that any injury is done to society by the evil thought; but there is no question that it will be stigmatised as an injustice; and the offender himself, in another frame of mind, is often ready enough to admit that he has failed to be just towards his neighbour. However, it may plausibly be said, that so slight a barrier lies between thought and speech, that any moral quality attached to the latter is easily transferred to the former; and that, since open slander is obviously opposed to the interests of society, injustice of thought, which is silent slander, must become inextricably associated with the same blame.

But, granting the utility to society of all kinds of benevolence and justice, why should the quality of those virtues involve the sense of moral obligation?

Hume answers this question in the fifth section, entitled, Why Utility Pleases. He repudiates the deduction of moral approbation from self-love, and utterly denies that we approve of benevolent or just actions because we think of the benefits which they are likely to confer indirectly on ourselves. The source of the approbation with which we view an act useful to society must be sought elsewhere; and, in fact, is to be found in that feeling which is called sympathy.

"No man is absolutely indifferent to the happiness and misery of others. The first has a natural tendency to give pleasure, the second pain. This every one may find in himself. It is not probable that these principles can be resolved into principles more simple and universal, whatever attempts may have been made for that purpose."--(IV. p. 294, Note.)

Other men's joys and sorrows are not spectacles at which we remain unmoved:--

" ... The view of the former, whether in its causes or effects, like sunshine, or the prospect of well-cultivated plains (to carry our pretensions no higher) communicates a secret joy and satisfaction; the appearance of the latter, like a lowering cloud or barren landscape, throws a melancholy damp over the imagination. And this concession being once made, the difficulty is over; and a natural unforced interpretation of the phenomena of human life will afterwards, we hope, prevail among all speculative inquirers."--(IV. p. 320.)

The moral approbation, therefore, with which we regard acts of justice or benevolence rests upon their utility to society, because the perception of that utility or, in other words, of the pleasure which they give to other men, arouses a feeling of sympathetic pleasure in ourselves. The feeling of obligation to be just, or of the duty of justice, arises out of that association of moral approbation or disapprobation with one's own actions, which is what we call conscience. To fail in justice, or in benevolence, is to be displeased with oneself. But happiness is impossible without inward self-approval; and, hence, every man who has any regard to his own happiness and welfare, will find his best reward in the practice of every moral duty. On this topic Hume expends much eloquence.

"But what philosophical truths can be more advantageous to society than these here delivered, which represent virtue in all her genuine and most engaging charms, and make us approach her with ease, familiarity, and affection? The dismal dress falls off, with which many divines and some philosophers have covered her; and nothing appears but gentleness, humanity, beneficence, affability; nay, even at proper intervals, play, frolic, and gaiety. She talks not of useless austerities and rigours, suffering and self-denial. She declares that her sole purpose is to make her votaries, and all mankind, during every period of their existence, if possible, cheerful and happy; nor does she ever willingly part with any pleasure but in hopes of ample compensation in some other period of their lives. The sole trouble which she demands is that of just calculation, and a steady preference of the greater happiness. And if any austere pretenders approach her, enemies to joy and pleasure, she either rejects them as hypocrites and deceivers, or if she admit them in her train, they are ranked, however, among the least favoured of her votaries.

"And, indeed, to drop all figurative expression, what hopes can we ever have of engaging mankind to a practice which we confess full of austerity and rigour? Or what theory of morals can ever serve any useful purpose, unless it can show, by a particular detail, that all the duties which it recommends are also the true interest of each individual? The peculiar advantage of the foregoing system seem to be, that it furnishes proper mediums for that purpose."--(IV. p. 360.)

In this paen to virtue, there is more of the dance measure than will sound appropriate in the ears of most of the pilgrims who toil painfully, not without many a stumble and many a bruise, along the rough and steep roads which lead to the higher life.

Virtue is undoubtedly beneficent; but the man is to be envied to whom her ways seem in anywise playful. And, though she may not talk much about suffering and self-denial, her silence on that topic may be accounted for on the principle va sans dire. The calculation of the greatest happiness is not performed quite so easily as a rule of three sum; while, in the hour of temptation, the question will crop up, whether, as something has to be sacrificed, a bird in the hand is not worth two in the bush; whether it may not be as well to give up the problematical greater happiness in the future, for a certain great happiness in the present, and

"Buy the merry madness of one hour With the long irksomeness of following time."[46]

If mankind cannot be engaged in practices "full of austerity and rigour," by the love of righteousness and the fear of evil, without seeking for other compensation than that which flows from the gratification of such love and the consciousness of escape from debasement, they are in a bad case. For they will assuredly find that virtue presents no very close likeness to the sportive leader of the joyous hours in Hume's rosy picture; but that she is an awful Goddess, whose ministers are the Furies, and whose highest reward is peace.

It is not improbable that Hume would have qualified all this as enthusiasm or fanaticism, or both; but he virtually admits it:--

"Now, as virtue is an end, and is desirable on its own account, without fee or reward, merely for the immediate satisfaction which it conveys, it is requisite that there should be some sentiment which it touches; some internal taste or feeling, or whatever you please to call it, which distinguishes moral good and evil, and which embraces the one and rejects the other.

"Thus the distinct boundaries and offices of reason and of taste are easily ascertained. The former conveys the knowledge of truth and falsehood: The latter gives the sentiment of beauty and deformity, vice and virtue. The one discovers objects as they really stand in nature, without addition or diminution: The other has a productive faculty, and gilding and staining all natural objects with the colours borrowed from internal sentiment, raises in a manner a new creation. Reason being cool and disengaged, is no motive to action, and directs only the impulse received from appetite or inclination, by showing us the means of attaining happiness or avoiding misery. Taste, as it gives pleasure or pain, and thereby constitutes happiness or misery, becomes a motive to action, and is the first spring or impulse to desire and volition. From circumstances and relations known or supposed, the former leads us to the discovery of the concealed and unknown. After all circumstances and relations are laid before us, the latter makes us feel from the whole a new sentiment of blame or approbation. The standard of the one, being founded on the nature of things, is external and inflexible, even by the will of the Supreme Being: The standard of the other, arising from the internal frame and constitution of animals, is ultimately derived from the Supreme Will, which bestowed on each being its peculiar nature, and arranged the several classes and orders of existence."--(IV. pp. 376-7.)

Hume has not discussed the theological theory of the obligations of morality, but it is obviously in accordance with his view of the nature of those obligations. Under its theological aspect, morality is obedience to the will of God; and the ground for such obedience is two-fold; either we ought to obey God because He will punish us if we disobey Him, which is an argument based on the utility of obedience; or our obedience ought to flow from our love towards God, which is an argument based on pure feeling and for which no reason can be given. For, if any man should say that he takes no pleasure in the contemplation of the ideal of perfect holiness, or, in other words, that he does not love God, the attempt to argue him into acquiring that pleasure would be as hopeless as the endeavour to persuade Peter Bell of the "witchery of the soft blue sky."

In whichever way we look at the matter, morality is based on feeling, not on reason; though reason alone is competent to trace out the effects of our actions and thereby dictate conduct. Justice is founded on the love of one's neighbour; and goodness is a kind of beauty. The moral law, like the laws of physical nature, rests in the long run upon instinctive intuitions, and is neither more nor less "innate" and "necessary" than they are. Some people cannot by any means be got to understand the first book of Euclid; but the truths of mathematics are no less necessary and binding on the great mass of mankind. Some there are who cannot feel the difference between the Sonata Appassionata, and Cherry Ripe; or between a gravestone-cutter's cherub and the Apollo Belvidere; but the canons of art are none the less acknowledged. While some there may be, who, devoid of sympathy are incapable of a sense of duty; but neither does their existence affect the foundations of morality. Such pathological deviations from true manhood are merely the halt, the lame, and the blind of the world of consciousness; and the anatomist of the mind leaves them aside, as the anatomist of the body would ignore abnormal specimens.

And as there are Pascals and Mozarts, Newtons and Raffaelles, in whom the innate faculty for science or art seems to need but a touch to spring into full vigour, and through whom the human race obtains new possibilities of knowledge and new conceptions of beauty: so there have been men of moral genius, to whom we owe ideals of duty and visions of moral perfection, which ordinary mankind could never have attained; though, happily for them, they can feel the beauty of a vision, which lay beyond the reach of their dull imaginations, and count life well spent in shaping some faint image of it in the actual world.

THE END

LONDON: R. CLAY, SONS, AND TAYLOR, BREAD STREET HILL.

FOOTNOTES:

[45] Family affection in the eighteenth century may have been stronger than In the nineteenth; but Hume's bachelor inexperience can surely alone explain his strange account of the suppositions of the marriage law of that day, and their effects. The law certainly abolished all division of possessions, but it did so by making the husband sole proprietor.

[46] Ben Jonson's Cynthia's Revels, act i.

CPSIA information can be obtained
at www.ICGtesting.com
Printed in the USA
LVHW081044260121
677531LV00032B/561